MONSTER

A Miracle Monocle Micro-Anthology

The editorial staff of *Miracle Monocle* is pleased to reveal the second volume of its micro-anthology series. This ongoing, innovative publishing initiative will employ digital publishing techniques to address underserved communities in the literary world. Our hope is to offer worthy voices a new platform for expression and to illuminate underexplored territories for our readers.

MONSTER

A *Miracle Monocle* Micro-Anthology

Miracle Monocle
Louisville, Kentucky

First Printing: 2021

ISBN-13: 978-1-7341233-1-9

Miracle Monocle
University of Louisville
414 Stevenson Hall
101 E. Centennial Walk
Louisville, KY 40208
louisville.edu/miraclemonocle

Ordering Information: Copies of this book are available via the *Miracle Monocle* website and other online vendors. Special discounts are available on quantity purchases by corporations, associations, educators, and others. For details, please contact the publisher at the above listed address.

U.S. trade bookstores and wholesalers: Please contact *Miracle Monocle* at the above listed address.

Editor's Note

This book was conceived and executed by the editorial staff of *Miracle Monocle*, an award-winning literary journal housed at the University of Louisville. Our efforts were made possible by the generous support of the University of Louisville, the College of Arts and Sciences, the Department of English, the Program in Creative Writing, and generous donors like you.

We'd like to thank all of the writers who shared their words with us; the response to our call for entries was marvelous and encouraging. We hope you keep creating monsters always and forever.

This book would not have been possible without the hard work and creative energies of our student editors, who are celebrated on our masthead. We feel compelled to note that they labored through a global pandemic to bring you this book.

Warmly,

Dr. Sarah Anne Strickley
Faculty Editor of *Miracle Monocle*

Miracle Monocle

Miracle Monocle is an online journal of innovative literary and visual art. Published bi-annually, the journal features poems, short stories, literary nonfiction, and a broad range of experimental works. The journal is staffed by a team of graduate and undergraduate editors who earn course credit for assisting in the production of our issues. A faculty editor guides the editorial process, and creative writing faculty consult on the growth of the journal. Previously unpublished and emerging writers are highly encouraged to submit. Please visit our archives to sample issues of the journal and read our submission guidelines. Information about supporting *Miracle Monocle* is also available online; all donations are tax deductible to the extent allowed by the law.

Website: www.louisville.edu/miraclemonocle
Twitter: @miracle_monocle
Facebook: @miraclemonocle
Instagram: @miraclemonocle

Table of Contents

Hiking

Eisuke Aikawa translated by Toshiya Kamei

Her husband had told her he'd be home before dark, but eight o'clock came and went and he still wasn't home.

Shoko wouldn't have minded if he had gone out to celebrate with his coworkers after hiking. However, it wasn't like him not to have called to give her a heads-up. Since around six, she'd repeatedly called and texted, but she'd received no response. She wanted to call his colleagues who were with him, but she didn't have their numbers.

Shoko felt at a loss while seated at the table. The *nikujaga* she'd cooked for dinner had gone cold, and the timer on the rice cooker kept ticking away. She flipped on the TV to distract herself, but she got annoyed by the high-pitched voice-over and entertainers' guffaws, so she turned it off right away.

It might have been a mistake not to have a wedding ceremony. If she'd sent out invitations and received replies, she'd have had their numbers. However, it was no use having second thoughts six years later. Besides, it was Shoko's idea to forgo a formal wedding.

It still got cold at night in April. Her hands had gone cold. The intense quiet of her apartment exacerbated her anxiety. Familiar objects such as the coffee mug and the remote control suddenly seemed unfamiliar, and the button she pressed to draw water into the bathtub sounded different from usual.

It was Wednesday when her husband told her that he'd climb Mt. Nanao with his coworkers on the weekend. As the company had gone through a busy season without a hitch, they had organized a hiking trip on the section chief's suggestion. Although her husband was far from being athletic, Mt. Nanao wasn't that high, and the trail was well maintained and it took only a couple of hours to go up to the top, so she had no reason to oppose it. Seven of them hiking together, there was no chance of getting lost. Her morning sickness finally under control, she had been lately able to eat what she wanted. She decided to order pizza and eat it alone while watching a horror movie her husband hated.

Should she call the police? Should she talk to Izawa sensei from the ink painting class? Shoko wandered around the room like a lost dog. She decided to wait fifteen more minutes. Perhaps she had misheard her husband. After all, she didn't want to make a fuss and embarrass him.

Yes, she'd heard him right.

He'd said he would eat dinner at home. She stepped out on the veranda and gazed outside, but her husband was nowhere to be seen. The streets were all dark. Her emotions ricocheting off every part of her mind, she struggled to keep herself calm.

She decided to call the police when the clock's hand pointed to ten. Then she heard the door unlock and open. Shoko dashed to the entrance.

"I'm home. So tired." Her husband's tired voice reached her.

"Oh, what happened to you?" Shoko asked.

Her husband was covered with soil, and his gray sweater was torn and frayed. A broken twig peaked from his jeans' pocket.

"Eh? You mean this?" Just then he seemed to have noticed something was amiss. His reaction lacked any sense of urgency.

"What happened?"

"I wonder if I dirtied Mr. Shibata's car."

"I don't care about that right now. Did you have trouble?"

"No, it's not that. I got lost up there." Her husband blushed as usual.

"Lost?"

"I spotted a rare butterfly on the way down, so I wanted to take a picture, but I dropped my phone. It rolled down to the bottom of a slope. So I told the others to go ahead without me and tried to go down, but I slipped and rolled down like a rice ball."

It was no laughing matter.

"I must've hit my head and passed out for a while. It was evening when I woke up."

"Are you all right, honey?"

"Of course I am."

"Why don't you go see a doctor?"

"Don't worry. Only the ER is open at this hour. I'd hate waiting in the waiting room for hours."

"But . . ."

"My joints were sore. I didn't find my phone. On top of it, a strange old man stole my backpack. What a day. I've had enough already."

"A strange old man?"

"Yeah. It was something else." His eyes shone suddenly.

"What do you mean?"

"After I regained my senses, I wandered around the area in search of my phone. I put down my backpack by a tree because it was heavy. When I walked around and came back, an old man in a shabby trench coat was rummaging through my backpack and gobbling up my biscuits. I was stunned. He showed up out of the blue. Must have been homeless or something. When I moved closer, he turned around. He had a strange face, no, rather strange eyes. I didn't want to get caught, so I ran like hell. I stumbled a few times and went down aimlessly, but I somehow ended up on the trail. Everyone was waiting at the bottom. I apologized for making them worry."

"Did you lose your backpack?"

"Well, doesn't matter now. I had my wallet in my pocket, so I don't mind losing the rest. Let's eat. I'm hungry."

"What about your phone?"

"I'll buy a new one tomorrow."

"Is your head really OK?" Shoko stopped her husband as he removed his shoes and entered the corridor.

"If I feel bad, I'll tell you know right away. Is that all right? What about you, Shoko? You look pale. What's the matter?"

Whose fault was that?

"Yeah, I got a little cold while I was waiting."

"That's no good. What if something happens to the baby? You should take a bath right away and keep yourself warm."

"No, you go first. You must be tired."

"A bath can wait. I'm starving."

"But— "

"You go ahead." Her husband began to sound irritated.

"Okay. I'll heat up the food right away."

"I can just microwave it. Hurry up and take a bath."

She still had many more questions she wanted to ask, but she decided to go along with her husband. She didn't want any argument.

When she immersed herself in the hot water, a tingling, numbing sensation crept up. Her whole body became loose. She dipped her mouth beneath the water's surface and let out bubbles of air.

When she returned to the living room in her pajamas, her husband was eating in silence. He didn't seem to notice her. He didn't even look up. He must have been hungry. Shoko smiled at her husband as she found him somewhat boyish.

She went closer and gasped.

He hadn't left her anything. Although the food wasn't divided into two portions, it was obviously for both of them. He's got nerve, she thought, devouring everything like a starving hyena. When she opened the rice cooker, there was almost no rice left.

She was too amazed to be angry. Never had she imagined that he could be so thoughtless.

Her husband put down his chopsticks and looked up. "Can you give me something sweet?" he asked. Hadn't he had enough?

Shoko took out a chocolate bar from a cupboard shelf and handed it to him. He ripped off the wrapping paper and gobbled down the whole bar, smearing chocolate all over his lips. Still seemingly unsatisfied, he rummaged through the fridge and slobbered over an ice cream cup. Shoko was now afraid.

"Let me take you to the hospital," she suggested as she grabbed his shoulders.

"What for?"

He didn't seem to be clueless. Shoko gave up explaining to her husband and hired a taxi without his consent. She changed into a jersey and wrapped herself in a thin jacket.

She pushed her husband into the back seat and headed to the largest emergency hospital in the area.

The CT exam found no abnormalities. They arrived home late at night. "I told there was nothing wrong with me." Her husband became sullen.

Emotional ups and downs exhausted her. Because she'd lost her appetite, she crawled into bed while her husband was taking a bath. She fell asleep right away.

She had a nightmare. In her dream, shapeless amoeba-like creatures stuck to her skin.

She woke up to the hum of the microwave.

When she groped beneath the covers next to her, she didn't find her husband.

The digital clock showed it was past three in the morning. As she walked toward the kitchen, she heard someone slurping noodles in the dark.

When she turned the light on, she saw her husband seated at the table. Instant fried noodles spilled out of his mouth. Shoko stood stunned, frozen to the spot. A loaf of bread, frozen fried rice, and a gift pack of ham from her parents. Various food packages were scattered on the table. Even an apple core lay among them. The room was filled with a stifling foul odor.

Her husband cast a beastly glance at her, but when he realized it was his wife, he returned to his usual self.

"Oh, I'm so hungry for some reason," her husband explained with an embarrassed smile.

He'd eaten a lot. That should have been enough. She tried to say that aloud, but a lump clogged her throat.

"Don't give me that look," he said while he kept shoveling food into his mouth with his chopsticks. Just watching him made her nauseated.

Shoko wanted to believe she was still dreaming. She turned around and closed the door when she returned to the bedroom. Even when she shut her eyes, she still saw her husband guzzling like a stray dog. She petted her belly and tried to calm herself with happy thoughts of the future. When she woke up in the morning, everything would be all right. She assured herself and tried to force herself to sleep.

However, she couldn't escape into the dream world and when she woke up, the problem was still there.

As dawn drew near, Shoko returned to the living room and found her husband lying on the floor, snoring with a peaceful look on his face. He reminded her of a catfish out of water. The amount of food he'd consumed had doubled, and jam jars and butter boxes were scattered around. Apparently, he had eaten them one by one. There was a lot of evidence around his mouth. He'd finished most of the food in the house. She was fond of her husband's boyish figure, his prominent rib cage, but he had ballooned overnight. His stomach had swelled up as if he were pregnant, too, moving up and down as he breathed.

Although they'd gone through some ups and downs, they had led a relatively quiet married life. With a baby on the way, Shoko was ready to enter a new stage of life, but never had she doubted her life would stay pretty much the same. But her expectations collapsed suddenly.

Tears welled up as she gazed at the man she now hardly recognized. She hurried to the bathroom and splashed water over her face. Her lips were cracked and dark bags were visible under her eyes. Shoko slapped her own cheeks twice. This was her reality now. She'd have to deal with it.

She booted up her computer in the study that was to be converted into a nursery and did a search for "bulimia." She took the time to peruse the sites that seemed relevant.

He had some bulimia-like symptoms such as out-of-control appetite, but he also exhibited other symptoms. If the symptoms matched exactly, she'd feel relieved. She did a search on "satiety center," but she couldn't come up with any clues.

Did something happen at work? She opened the homepage of the company where her husband worked and read it thoroughly, but she found nothing relevant. Then she combined words such as "hiking" and "sickness" in her online search. Still, she came up empty.

Then she did a search on Mt. Nanao. Even though she knew her search was futile, she couldn't let go of the mouse. She should probably take her husband to a reputable mental clinic right away. But she was too afraid to face her reality.

Hidarugami.

Shoko's hand froze. A mystery at Mt. Nanao. Said to have lived there since the Edo period, Hidarugami cast a spell on hikers lost in the depths of the mountain and made them feel extremely hungry.

While she stared at the computer screen, her husband barged into the room. Shoko closed the page in a hurry.

"Good morning." He held a bag of crackers. He stuck his hand into the bag, grabbed a handful, and shoved them into his mouth.

"That's for an emergency." Shoko took the bag away from him.

"But I'm hungry." Her husband pouted like a small boy.

"You've had enough already."

"What do you mean?"

"Look at the mess in the living room."

"So what? I want my breakfast now."

You've eaten all the bread for breakfast. She stopped herself from saying it aloud. She knew it would fall on deaf ears.

Shoko pushed her husband aside, headed to the bedroom, and locked the door behind her. She wanted to go back to sleep, but that wouldn't help. A visit to a mental clinic wouldn't help either. She'd have to act on her own to overcome the situation. She slid open the closet door and picked a high-necked sweater and a down jacket, even though it was late April. She put on maternity jeans, which were loose around her stomach.

While she changed, her husband begged for more food from the other side of the door. As he raised his voice, the knocking became louder.

It was Hidarugami. Despite not having any evidence at all, Shoko was sure of it now. Like an earthquake in the deep sea, no one noticed it. His gaze in the living room at midnight belonged to a madman. He had to be possessed by a monster.

According to the site she had consulted, a possessed person would die in a worst-case scenario. She had to do something about it as soon as possible.

She opened the door and shoved her husband away as he clung to her. She took a knife out of a drawer in the kitchen and put it in her purse. Her husband followed her like a poorly trained dog, so she scattered all the uncooked rice grains from the fridge. He scooped them into his hand and chewed them noisily. She packed her bag and left the apartment.

Although it had been a long while since she last got behind the wheel, she navigated through the streets without a major incident. She headed toward Mt. Nanao following the GPS directions.

As she got off the main road, she began to climb up a mountain road. She passed the parking lot at the trailhead and headed for the top. She turned the wheel hard into a curve, as if playing a video game. She boldly overtook the red Kei car ahead.

She parked at a small observation deck. Several couples savored the view. Her husband had brought her here shortly after they began going out on dates. It felt like a long time ago.

She had trouble finding the entrance to the mountain. Shoko was going to go down from the top. The couples' laughter bothered her.

What was her husband doing now? He had eaten all the food in the apartment. She'd brought his wallet, his keys, and all his shoes because she wouldn't want him to go out in his current state. If he had a smidgen of reason left, he would stay put. If she left him alone for a while, he might die of starvation.

After she wandered around for a while, she came across an animal trail. She took out the knife and cleaved through the thick grass, feeling like the knife-wielding maniac from the horror movie she had watched the day before.

She trod with great caution so as to keep her from slipping. The plants had grown as tall as Shoko's height, blocking her view and hindering her advance. Every direction was filled with dark green, and she felt herself increasingly diluted. Frustrated with her turtle-like pace, she snapped a tree branch. Insects smaller than mosquitoes swarmed around her ears and eyes in a gray fog. When an enormous millipede scurried near her feet, Shoko let out a brief scream.

She started having second thoughts about the whole idea. The mountain was completely different from her daily world. Hiking without being fully equipped was folly. But it was too late. The fuse had been lit. She had crossed over the point of no return.

She climbed down at a deliberate pace. Hidarugami could be lurking anywhere. Even though the mountain wasn't high, it was impossible to explore every inch of it on her own. She speed dialed her husband's number from time to time, but she heard no ringtone. Unfortunately, she'd have to rely on luck.

All sweaty, she was seized with a terrible thirst. She felt as if the fresh plants deprived her body of moisture. She should have at least brought a bottle of water. Her feet felt numb and fatigue began to weigh heavily on her as if gravity had increased its pull.

When she put her hand in her pocket, something rustled inside. It was a bag of crackers. Come to think of it, she hadn't eaten anything since noon the day before. Even though she was hungry, she didn't think dry crackers would pass down her dry throat.

Visibility had improved a bit. It wasn't a path regular hikers would visit, but it was a lot better than before. Where am I? she wondered.

She pressed the redial button again, even though she'd pretty much given up on finding her husband's phone. She didn't remember how many times she had called. "I can't find anything anyway. I'd better give up and go home before getting lost." Shoko let out a deep sigh. Silence. She couldn't even hear the wind swaying the plants and tree branches.

No, wait a minute.

She noticed something vibrating not so far away.

When Shoko looked closer, she spotted an orange backpack. She struggled to climb down the slope, slipping on the fern, but she grabbed the backpack. Someone had ransacked its contents, but no doubt it belonged to her husband. She found a plastic bottle and drank up the stale soda inside in one gulp.

Where was his phone? Shoko searched again inside the backpack, but to no avail.

When Shoko looked up, she saw a man standing nearby. He made no noise, so she detected no sign of his approach. She clapped her hands over her mouth to hold back her scream. A sullied trench coat, uncut hair, and unfocused eyes. Shoko immediately understood she now faced Hidarugami. She was surprised, but she never panicked.

The man stared at her. She told herself not to look him in the eye. Shoko took out the crackers from her pocket and dropped them at his feet. All of a sudden, Hidarugami groaned and crawled toward her.

Shoko plunged her knife into the nape of the man's neck. It felt as if she had stabbed something hard like a pumpkin. His blood splashed across her face. But it didn't faze her one bit. She pulled out the blade, shifted all her weight forward, and stabbed him again. As he fell down, she repeatedly stabbed his back and arms. Again and again and again. She repeated it mechanically until the man stopped moving.

How easy it was. Shoko thought while she breathed hard. Both of her hands were covered with blood. She slowly loosened her hardened grip. Hidarugami didn't scream at all. She never imagined she would come across the monster so easily. Her strong feelings must have attracted Hidarugami.

She felt his coat and found her husband's phone in the pocket. And something else. It was a discolored bi-fold wallet. It wasn't her husband's. Perhaps it once belonged to one of the other victims the monster had attacked. She checked the contents and found some coins and cards. A driver's license. Shoji Nakatsuka. Born in 1955. The photo somewhat resembled Hidarugami.

Shoko dragged the corpse into thick bushes and covered it with leaves, branches, and dirt. She took off her bloody down jacket and threw the wallet under the slope. After that, she felt the sudden urge to have a bowel movement. She wasn't able to hold back any longer, so she used some bushes as a toilet. She passed a stool so hard that she didn't need toilet paper.

She traced her way back through the broken branches and trampled grass. Out of energy, she needed to rest several times. Sweat mixed with blood streamed down her face. Her stomach felt heavy. She kept climbing, but she couldn't get to the exit. She felt space-time had been distorted, as if she had been walking for decades. By the time she had reached home, her husband might be an old man.

When she reached the observatory, the sun had already sunk behind the ridge. She collapsed into the driver's seat. As she fought off the urge to fall asleep, she mustered up the energy and turned the ignition key. When she glanced at the digital clock inside the car, it was already seven-thirty.

She grazed the guardrail a few times on the downhill. Her head felt heavy and her senses felt numb, as if she had taken a potent cold medicine. She tried to blink and shake herself awake as she began to nod off every few seconds.

When she returned to the main road, she felt relieved. She parked outside a convenience store nearby and went inside. She grabbed three pieces of stuffed bread and a bottle of mineral water. When she checked out, the cashier was taken aback by her hands, but he didn't say anything.

Shoko drank the water in one gulp outside the store. When she tore open the wrapping of the bread, the aromas of corn and mayonnaise reached her nostrils. She gobbled up one after another, almost biting off her own fingers. For a moment, she was worried that she might have been possessed by Hidarugami, but the bread had sated her appetite.

She went inside the store again and bought pouch-packed meals and packets of frozen udon noodles. She added iced coffee to keep herself awake. At the cash register, the cashier averted his eyes.

When she returned to her apartment, her husband was sleeping in the fetal position in the bedroom. She tiptoed to the bathroom and took a shower. She washed her whole body and scrubbed any dirt and blood out from under her nails.

When she stepped into the living room, she collected scattered items in a trash bag. Combustibles, incombustibles, bottles, and plastic bottles. She wiped off the food residue on the floor. Even though she was exhausted, she felt better as the room became clean. At last, she washed the dishes that had piled up in the sink. She cleaned the kitchen knife she had taken with great care and placed it in a drainer. Everything looked the same as before. No, one more thing. Shoko placed her husband's phone on the table. She flung open the window to let in the night air.

After a while, her husband came out of the bedroom, rubbing his eyes.

"Good morning," Shoko said.

"Good morning? Or good night, rather."

"Yeah, you're right." Shoko smiled.

Her husband looked around the room.

"You haven't had dinner yet, have you? Do you want me to heat up something?"

"No thanks. I've had heartburn all evening."

"I see." Shoko chuckled.

"It's no laughing matter," her husband protested like a sulky child. "Hey, when did you get back?" he asked.

"About an hour ago," she answered.

"Where did you go?"

"Well—"

"Your class?"

"Yeah."

He didn't pursue the question any further. He let out a large yawn and petted Shoko's pregnant belly as usual.

"Cold, isn't it? Let me close it," Shoko said and went to the window.

Behind her, her husband said, "Thanks."

Excerpts from *The Strange and Malevolent Beings of the 21st Century*

Zack Bean

The Blevlyn (more commonly known as an Echo Mistress) is a humanoid monster that takes the form of a quiet young woman who uses a combination of flattery and demure giggling to lure men to a temporary lair. Once there, the Blevlyn sings a song that relaxes her victim, and then asks him questions that have no answers. She quietly repeats his replies while staring into his eyes until he attempts to kiss her, at which point she uses her remarkable strength to suck his tongue loose from his mouth, leaving him bloody and screaming. Some witnesses have said that the Blevlyn has a faint greenish glow—possibly bioluminescent—and unusually powdery skin. They are believed by some experts to be the reincarnated souls of women whose murders were never solved.

Nearly everyone is familiar with a victim of a Shell Ghoul (or Micrososias) which is not technically a ghoul but rather a class of doppleganger known as a transformation parasite. The Shell Ghoul is actually a small colony of creatures that enters their victim through the ear or nostril, makes its way to the brain, and studies their mind and behavior for up to three weeks. while beginning a colony that will eventually commandeer the victim's body and slowly eats the brain from the inside while carrying on the victim's day-to-day functions. The whole cycle takes about six months. What makes a Shell Ghoul colony remarkable is that when the cycle is over, the Shell Ghoul colony naturally cannibalizes itself, imperfectly copying its own mind and memory, and repeating the process so that the victim becomes less and less defined as they age.

Life after death is thus possible in one sense: the victim dies quickly but appears to slowly degrade for many years. Thus, friends and family of the victim may continue to know him and wonder what has happened, how their loved one gradually lost all of the characteristics that once defined them.

Shell Ghouls are almost impossible to detect because they are only a few nanometers in length. They smell of soured laundry, and when millions are gathered together they fill the air with a hum, not unlike the static that sits just beneath the voices on a car radio.

A Flurmstrot (or Drain Spirit) is an invisible spirit that occupies a gathering room and waits for the room to fill with people. It usually hides in high corners by wedging itself between walls and ceilings. It contains billowy limbs that spread like drapes to absorb psychic energy. It then siphons the psychic energy from the room and the people inside it, so that in a matter of moments the room is drained of something vital and imperceptible. Those inside the room often notice, and they may voice their confusion, but they rarely speak of such a spirit, for no one wants to attract its attention.

Should you find yourself in the company of a Drain Spirit, it's best to leave quietly and enter a new environment before attempting to regain psychic energy.

The Flurmstrot is generally considered an itinerant nuisance rather than a community threat, and has on occasion been beneficial in dispersing mobs.

An outbreak of Ira Involvus in Western Europe and the United States has brought the Fury Worm (as it's usually called in casual conversation among specialists) into the spotlight in recent years. The Fury Worm is thin as a hair but can grow up to three kilometers in length. They often wind themselves into the walls of old homes and apartment buildings, where they sense the heartbeats of lonely humans. A Fury Worm usually wriggles unnoticed into a host's anus during the night. They are said to be attracted to the blue light of television and computer screens. The Fury Worm causes physical discomfort that hosts can't locate, increasing their irritability; anyone hosting a fury worm is unlikely to be able to sit contently for more than a few moments at a time, as the worm is literally wound through their whole body multiple times, and likely using its own rather pointy head to poke at fear receptors in the host's brain. Current Research suggests that the Ira Involvus has an aversion to green tea.

The MalinK'alo (or Many-Hands Demon) is a hoverer lurking near train stations, state fairs, concerts, anywhere a crowd gathers anonymously. An expert at camouflage and mind games, he (or it, rather) often takes the form of a young or middle-aged man, though it has been known to manifest as a woman, a librarian, a child, and on at least two separate occasions in Seattle as a Labrador Retreiver. One cannot look into the face of the MalinK'alo without immediately forgetting the details of that face: Were those eyes the color of smoke? Was that salt and pepper stubble or a pair of thin spectacles? Bushy eyebrows or a nose that may have been broken in the past? It is impossible to recall the face, as it melts into other faces you may have seen. However, you do not forget the touch of a MalinK'alo: a firm, cold hand that seems to press through your clothes and chill your skin, and then the sensation that something has been taken from you. The hand of the MalinK'alo may first press against your thigh or your hip or the small of your back, but soon you feel it everywhere. That cold handprint lingers long after the face of the MalinK'alo has vanished into the crowd. And, although you may forget the touch in a day or two's time, it may return to you months or years from now in the early predawn hours, awakening you from a deep, dark dream that you cannot remember and sending an icy shudder through your body, reminding you that you are never truly alone.

The breath of the Noncorsouche (or Nothing Witch), although it smells of honey and woodland flowers, can leave a grown man in tears of despair. This witch is a double-thief: she first steals items of sentimental value from attics, basements, and storage units, and with these, she brews a potion that gives her magic breath. The more valued the goods were by their owners, the more potent the brew. She may leave her breath like a floating trap hovering over a hiking trail, or in an airplane terminal, or in the parking lot of a rest stop beside the interstate. There it stays, her breath, invisible molecules of air, just floating in a perfect cloud where she leaves them. She will hide nearby, waiting for some unlucky soul to breathe the cloud of breath she has left. When they do, she will whistle at a pitch nearly inaudible to human ears. This is when her second theft occurs. The breath, thus activated by the whistle, returns to the witch, bringing with it a significant portion of the life energy of the person who breathed it in. This is what gives the Nothing Witch her unusually long life. Victims of the Nothing Witch report that they feel an indescribable loss, like all of the value they once saw in the world has suddenly vanished. This is not the case, of course. It is they who have changed.

There is no point in looking out for the Noncorsouche. They come in all shapes and sizes, and by the time you have discovered one, it's too late, too late. The effects of this encounter may last from two weeks to three months. However, if you *kiss* a Noncorsouche, that's entirely another matter!

Hobbled

Jen Fawkes

The jay slices through your field of vision, bearing in her beak something squirmy to deliver to her nestlings, which hatched while you and Shane were barricaded in the house, blinds drawn, gripping plucked toilet paper tubes, chasing acrid plumes of smoke rising from aluminum foil squares, wondering who might be crouched in the overgrown azaleas, whether life exists on other planets, whether anyone else ever laughed so hard, which country artist might record your song. Shane stole the melody from the jay that built her nest in the crab apple outside Nadine's ramshackle bungalow, but when you point this out, he flies into a fury. Smashes his guitar, the acoustic Martin that belonged to his father, who roadied for Bocephus and came within a whisker of making it in Nashville. Seizes your slight shoulders, shakes you until your head lolls, until you see nothing but whipping lengths of unwashed hair and streaks of Shane—his straight, yellowing teeth, his etched brow. He slaps you twice, then withdraws to a corner to crouch, rock, and weep. You sink to the carpet and sit cross-legged, thinking how Nadine's previous boyfriends would have bloodied you for half as much—the Hell's Angel from Sarasota, the construction foreman from Bristol. *Pussy*, you say to Shane, but gently, and when he ventures out for more baking soda you perch backward on the sofa, blinds twisted open, begging Claxton Road for a glimpse of his returning pickup. He's been off and on with Nadine since you were fourteen, and like the others, he's stupid, but unlike them, he's tender. Cries like a child at the sight of anything crippled, broken, lame. He's never fucked you—not even when Nadine's passed out or missing in action, as she's been now for a week, not even when you've stripped for him, ground your downy crotch into his thigh, pleaded. He kisses the nape of your neck. Pulls you into his lap. Cradles you. Listens. As light soaks the firmament, you abandon the sofa, open the front door, penetrate the mist that cloaks the weedy yard, shimmy up the crab apple's rough trunk. You wear the red bra and purple panties you've had on for days, since Shane materialized on the porch, a glint in his eye, two eight balls stashed in his Jaguars windbreaker. You locate the nest, study the baby jays—five yellow beaks yawning like forsythia in bloom; membranous lids taut over bulgy eyes; flesh-toned, vein-mapped things awash in damp fuzz and blue-specked shell fragments. When Shane finds you there, when he discovers that you've methodically, tenderly snapped one of each chick's tiny wings, he'll tear at his hair, tears sliding down his sun-browned cheeks. *Why?* he'll say. *My God, Talley, why?* But it won't be possible to explain to him that you couldn't let the birds go. That if they flew away, they would take with them all that was left of your heart.

But Come Ye Back

Melanie Gillman

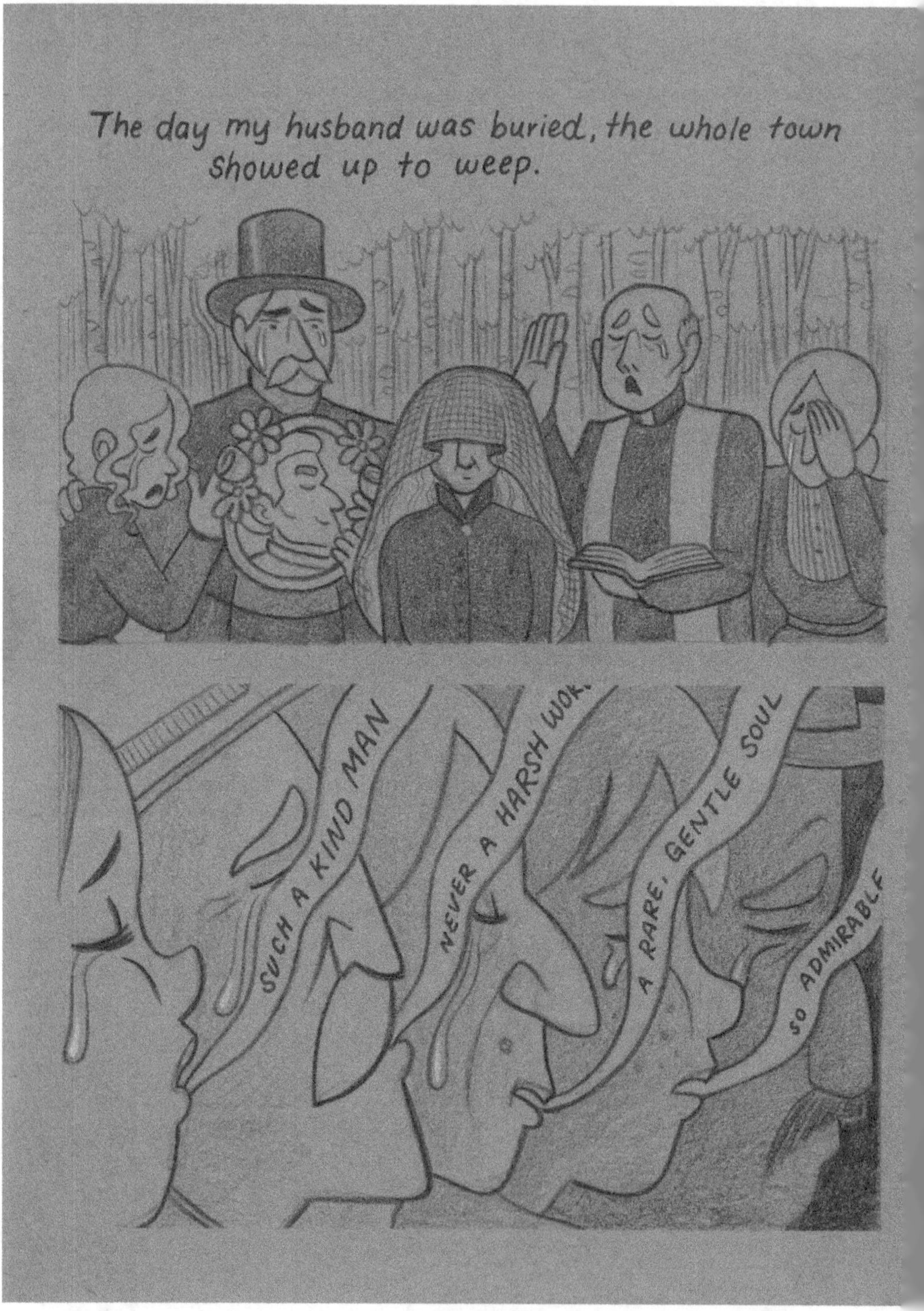

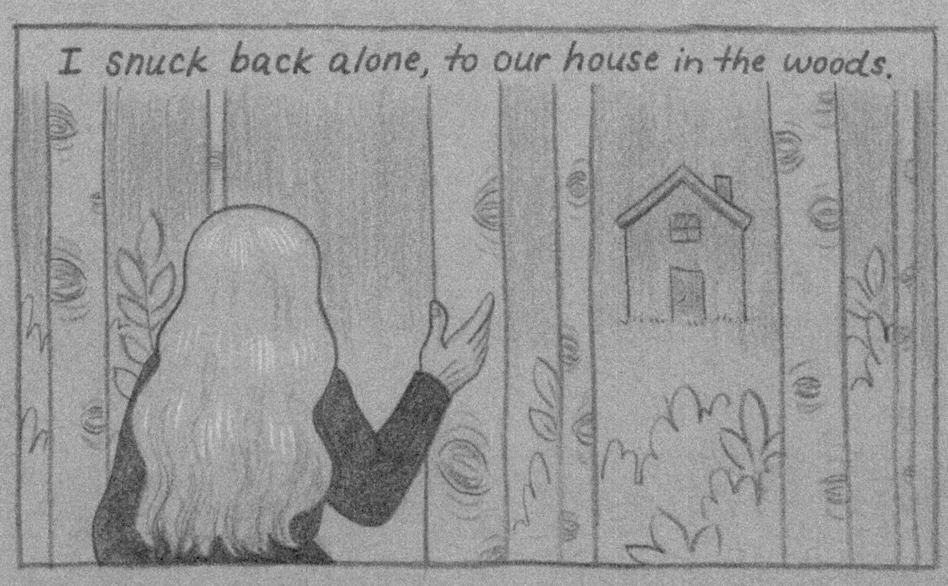
I snuck back alone, to our house in the woods.

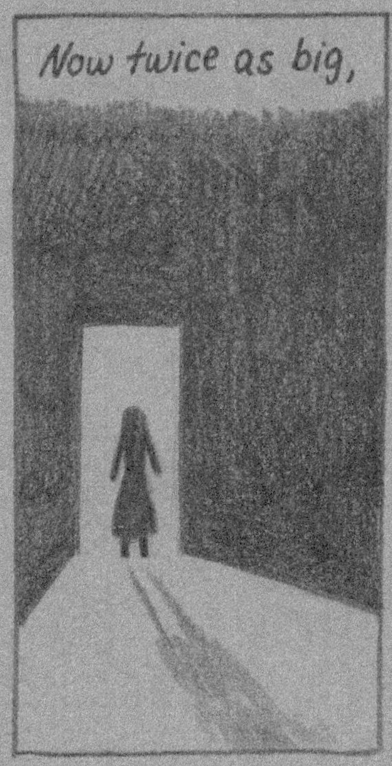
Now twice as big,

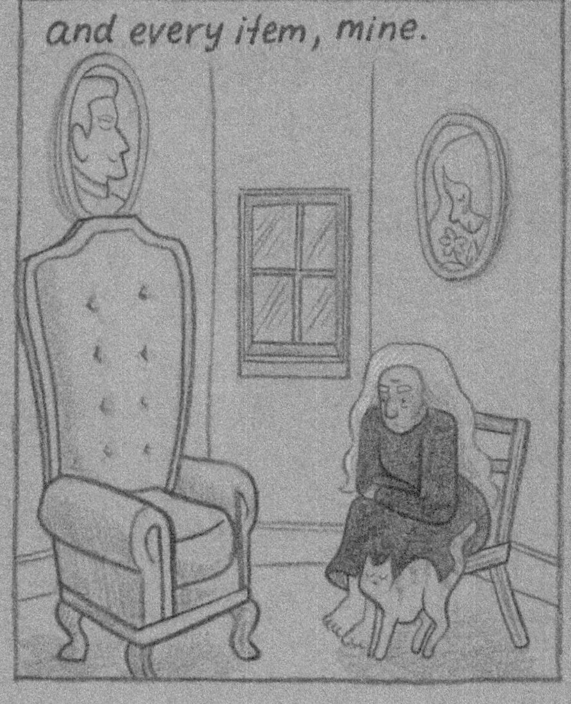
and every item, mine.

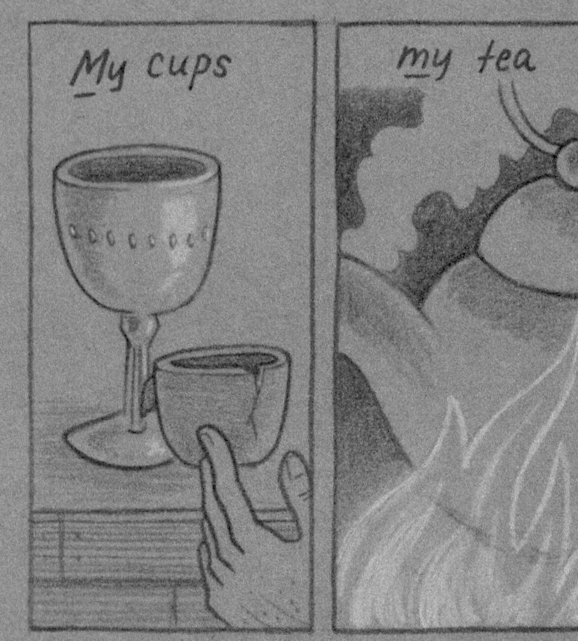
My cups
my tea

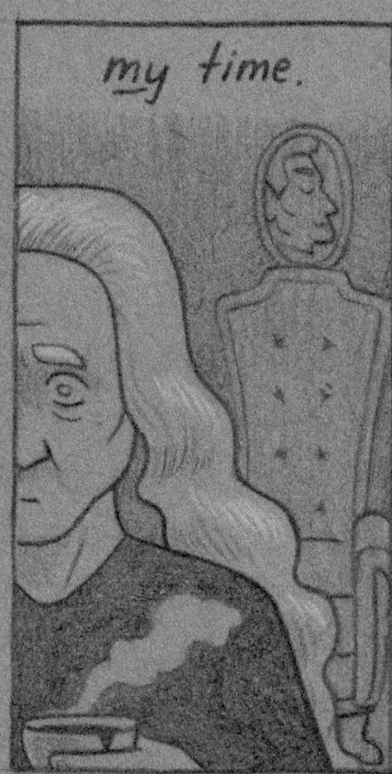
my time.

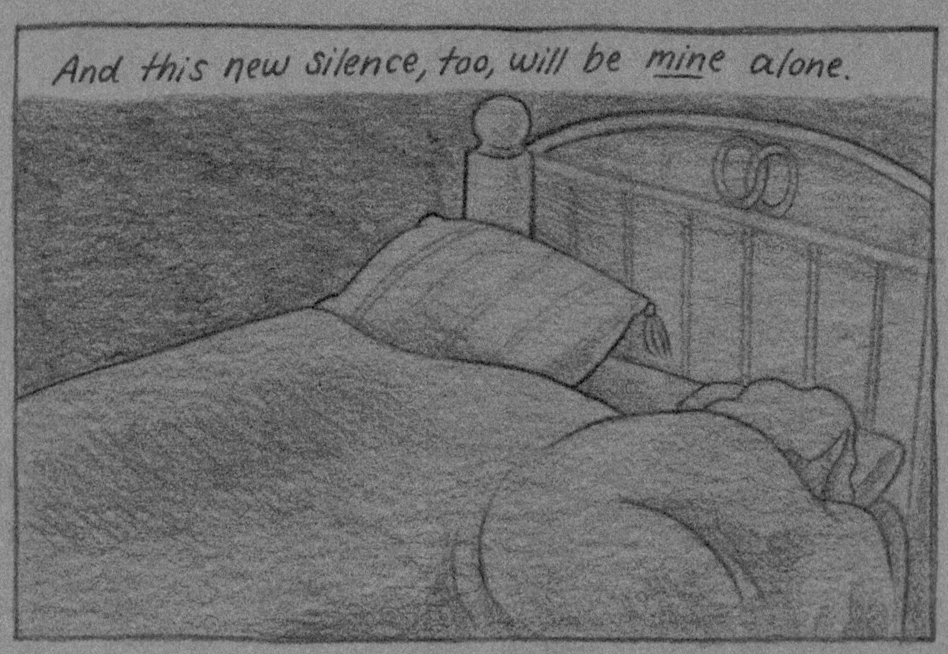
And this new silence, too, will be mine alone.

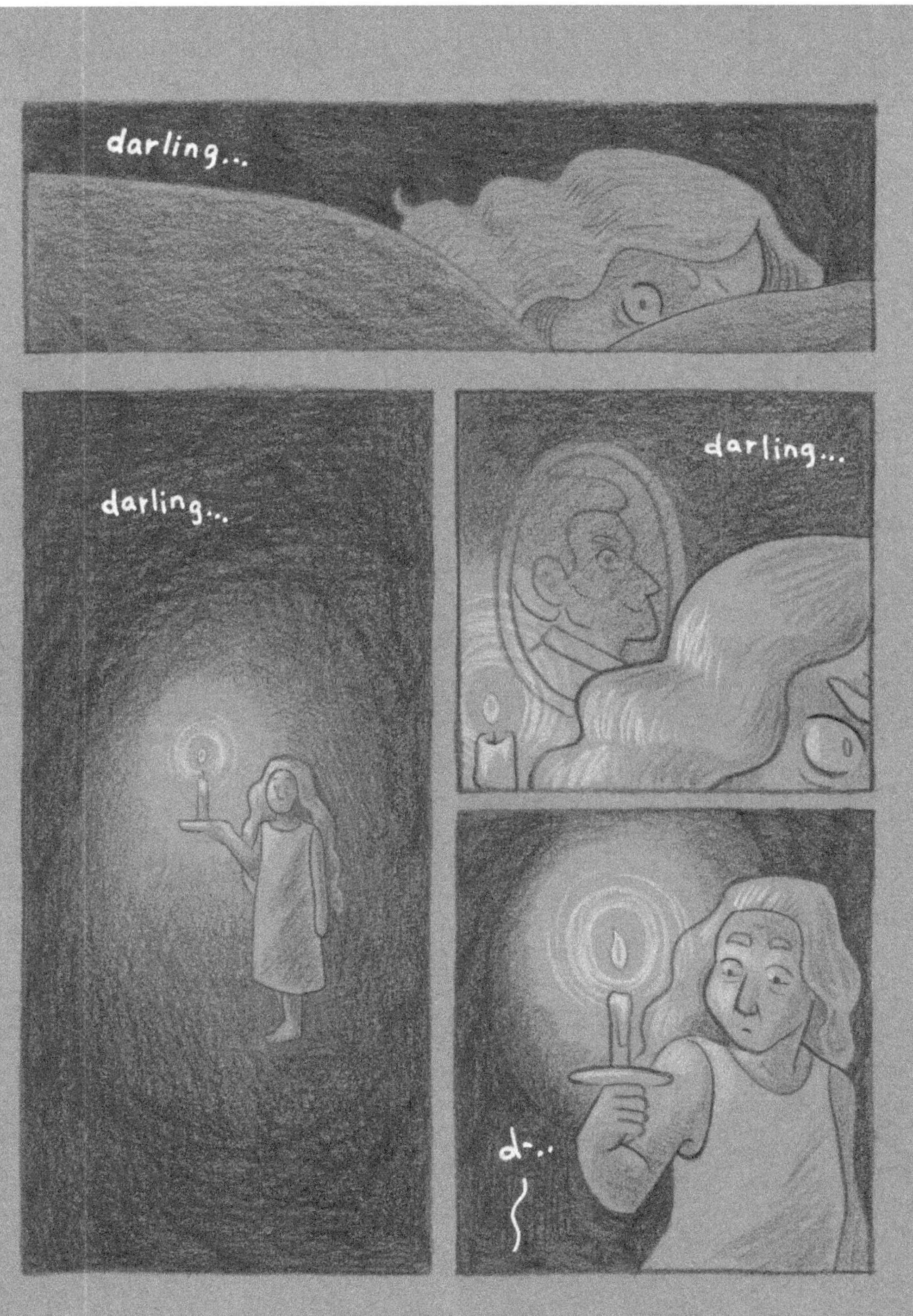
darling...
darling...
darling...
d-..

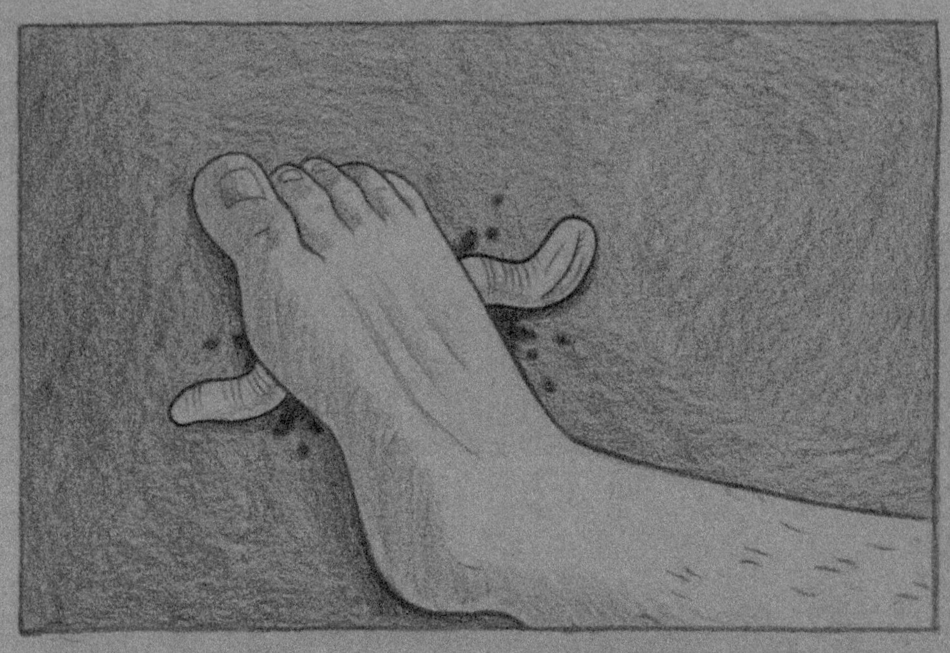

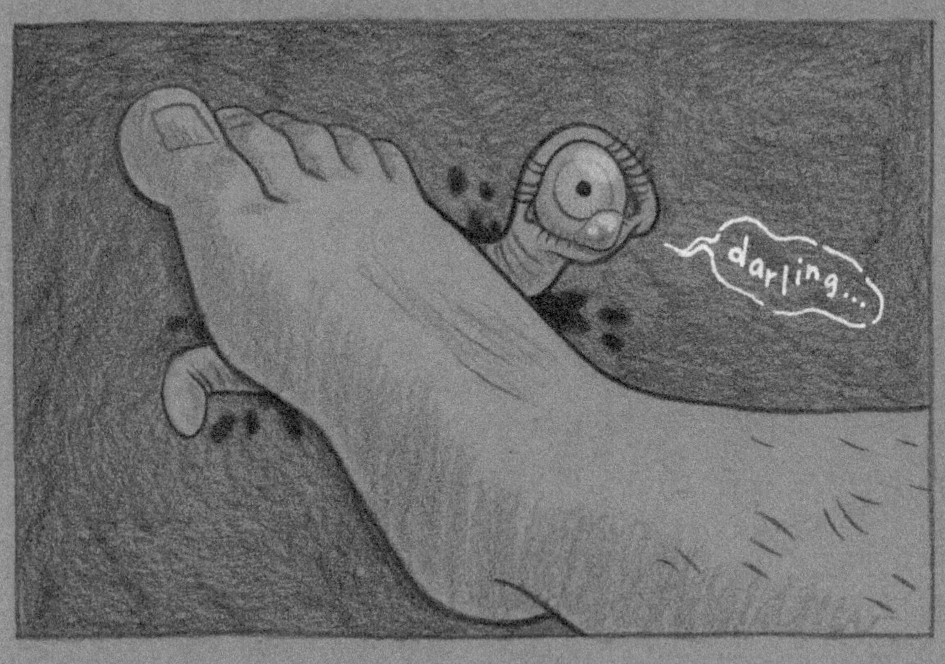
darling...

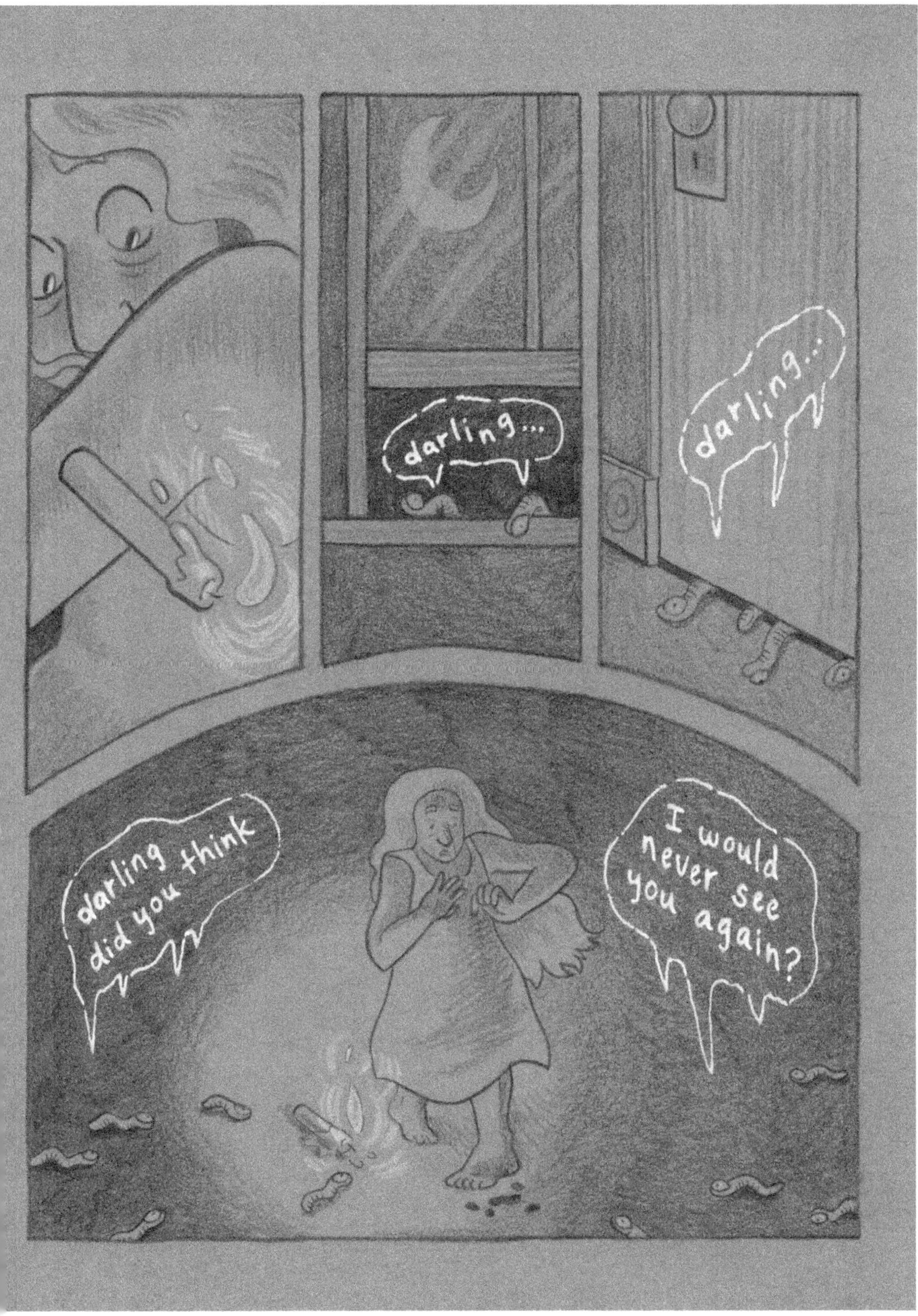
darling...
darling...
darling did you think
I would never see you again?

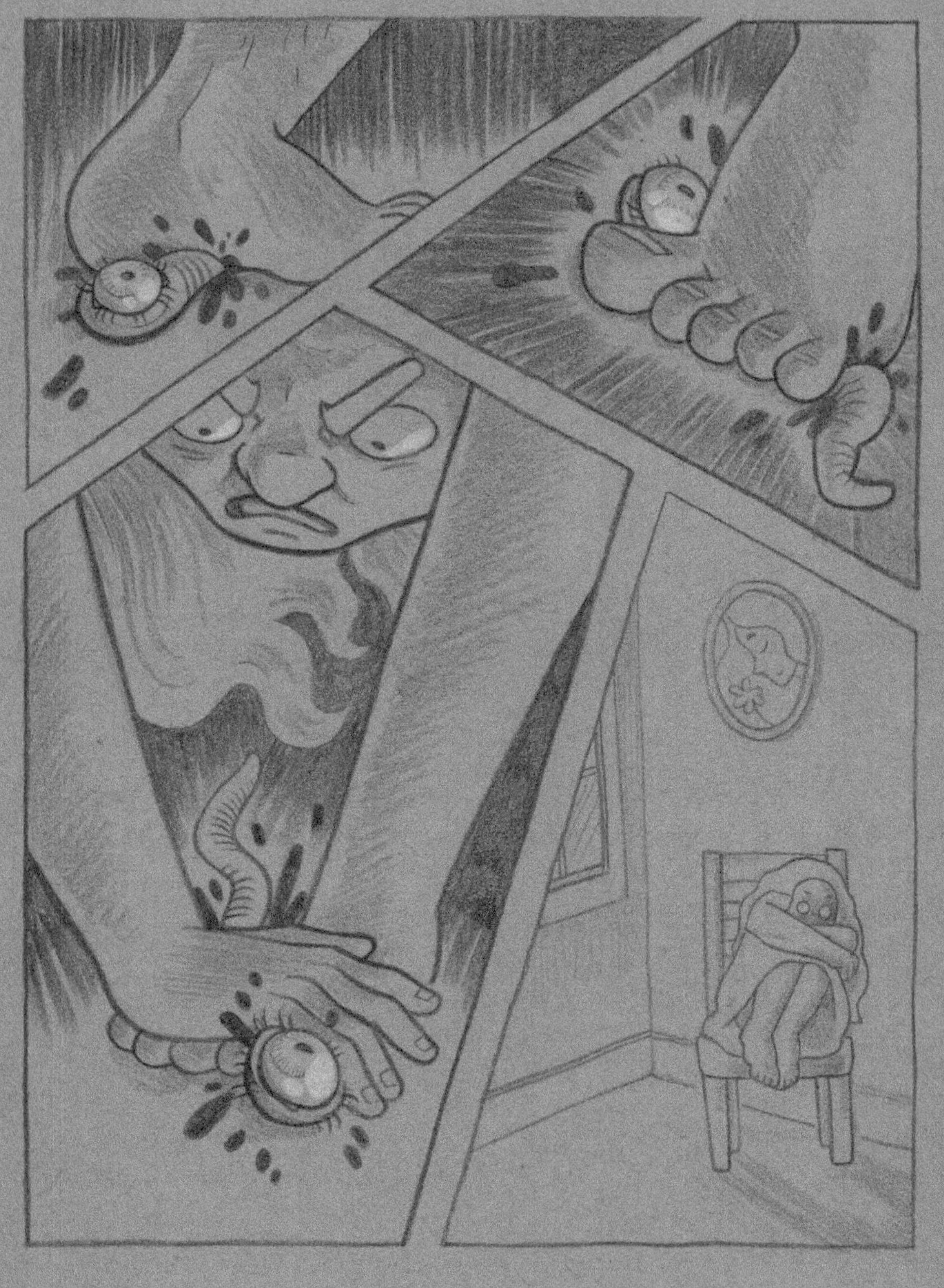

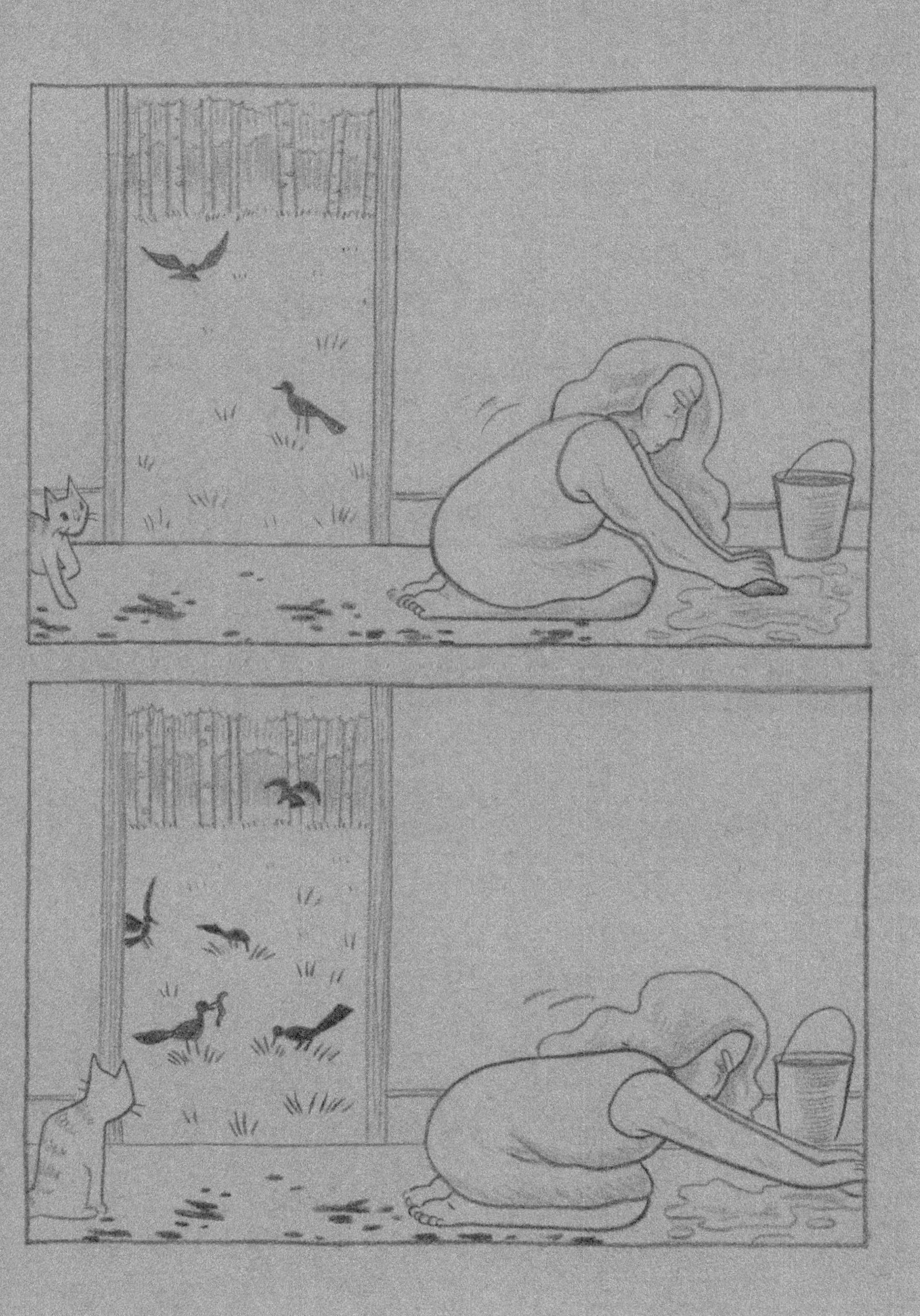

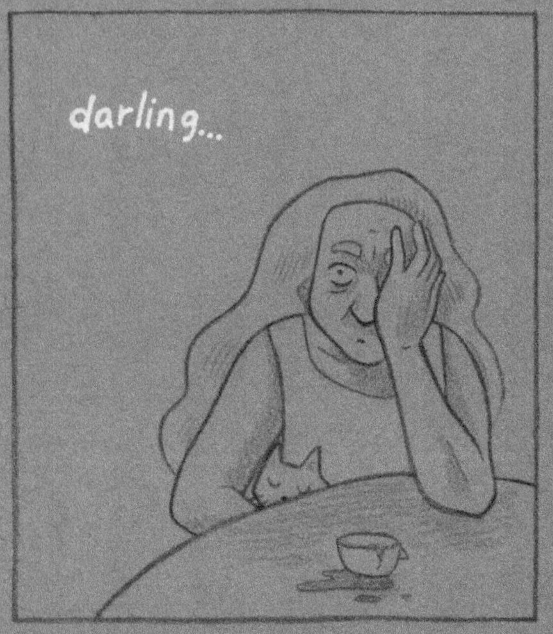
darling...

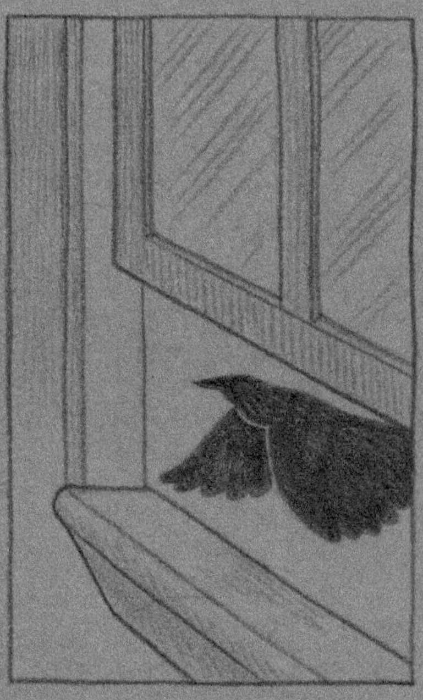

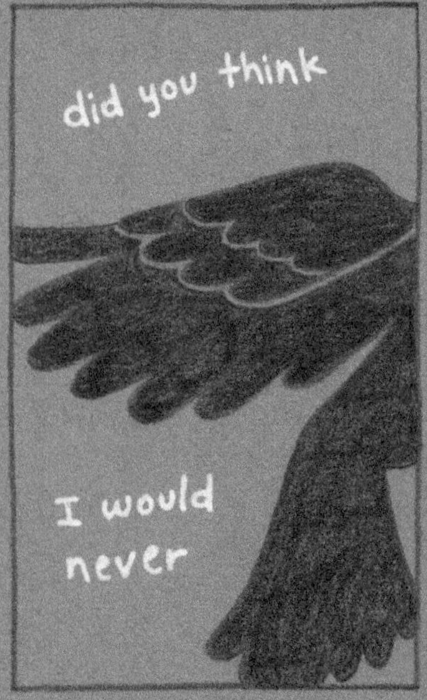
did you think
I would never

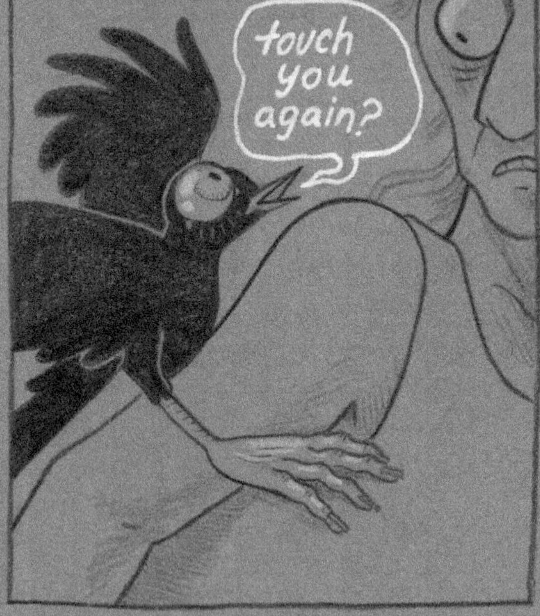
touch you again?

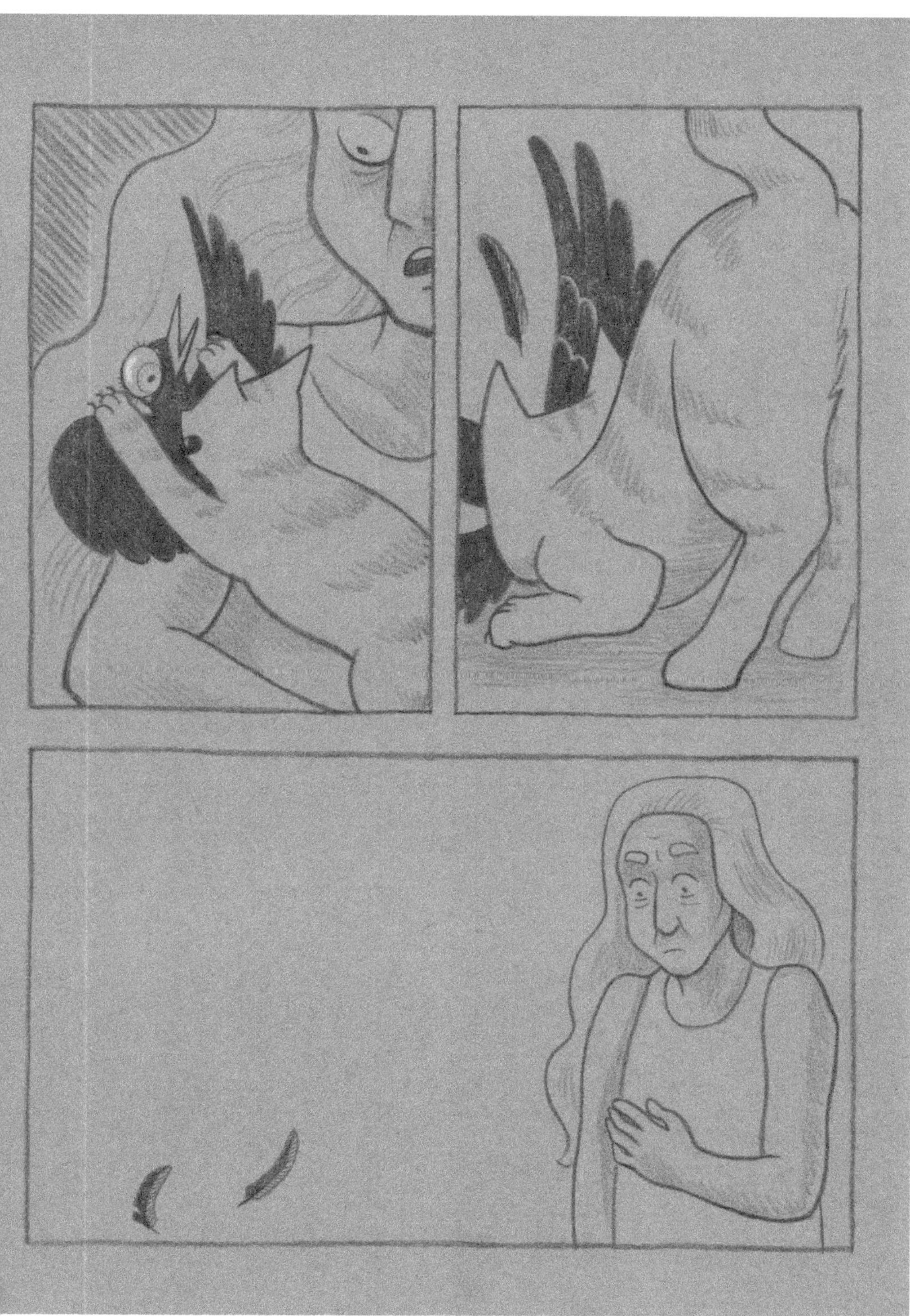

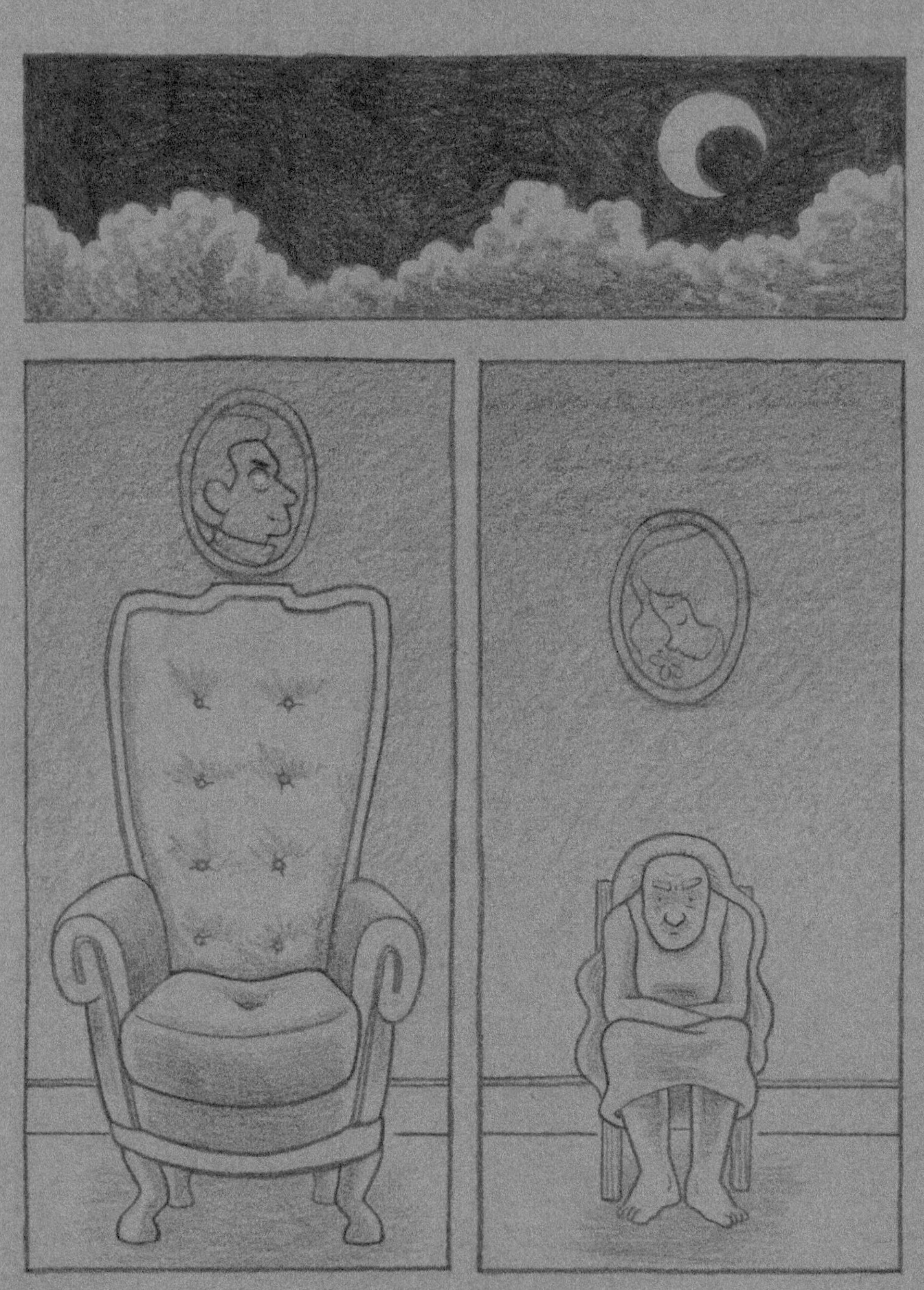

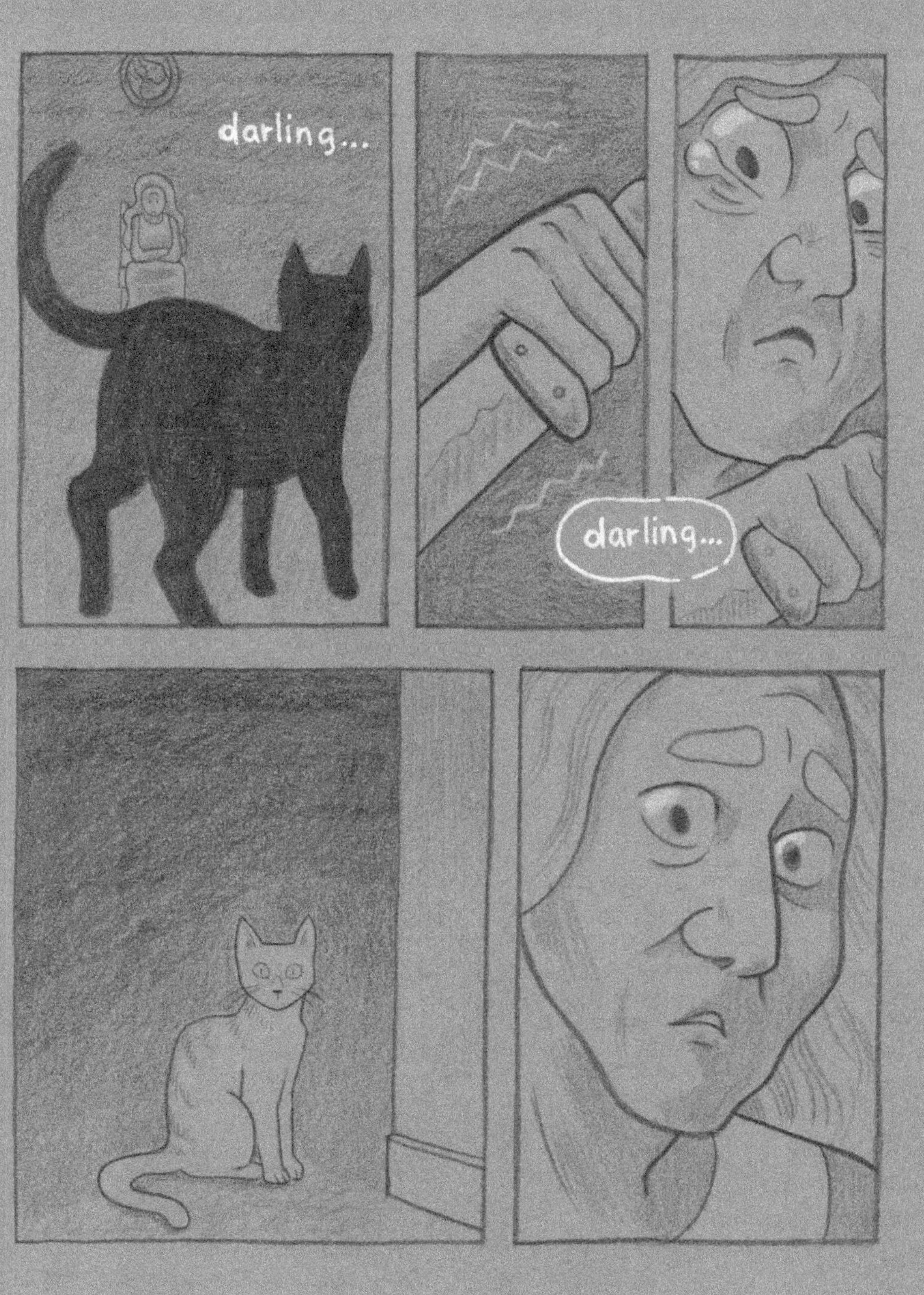
darling...
darling...

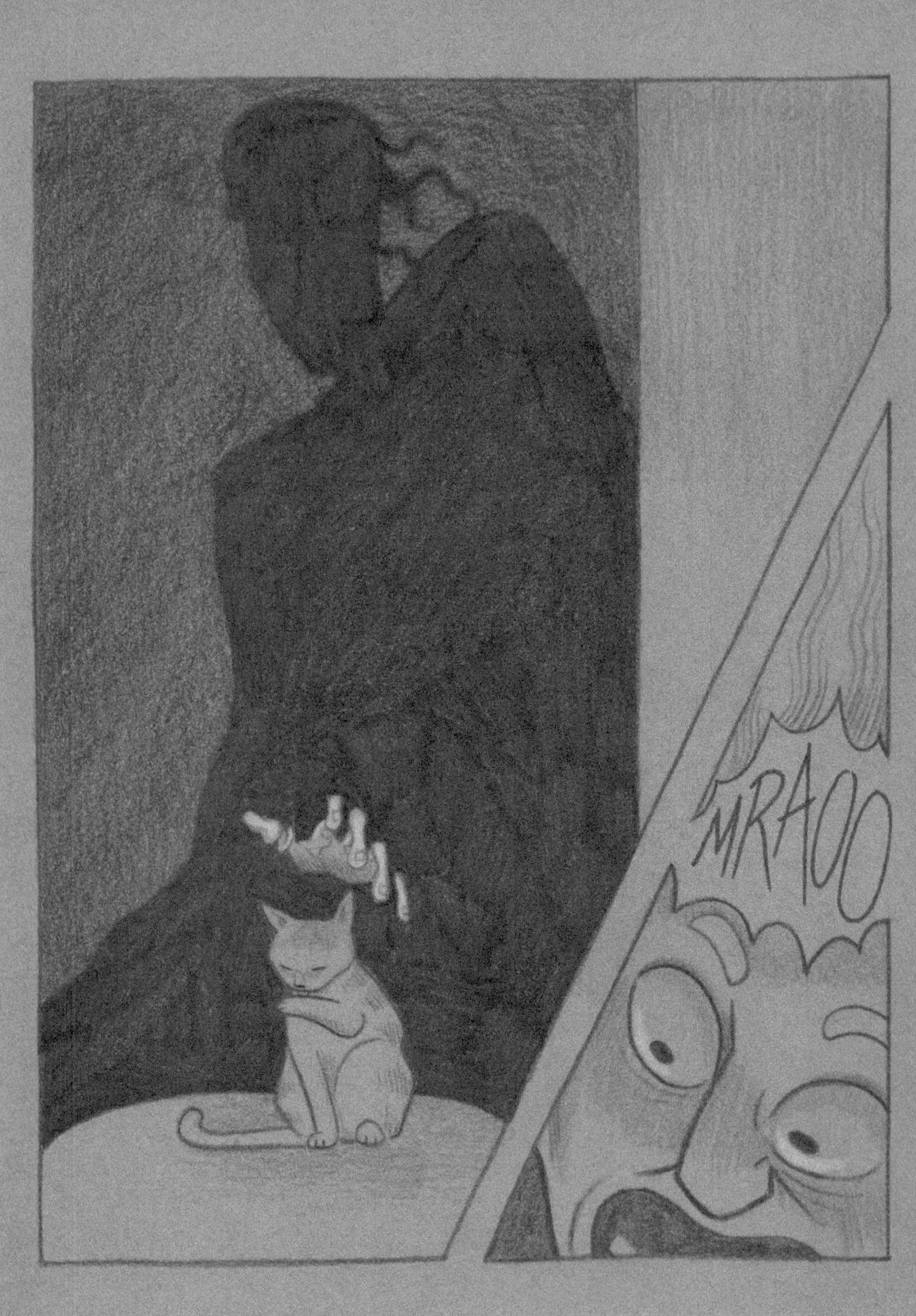
MRAOO

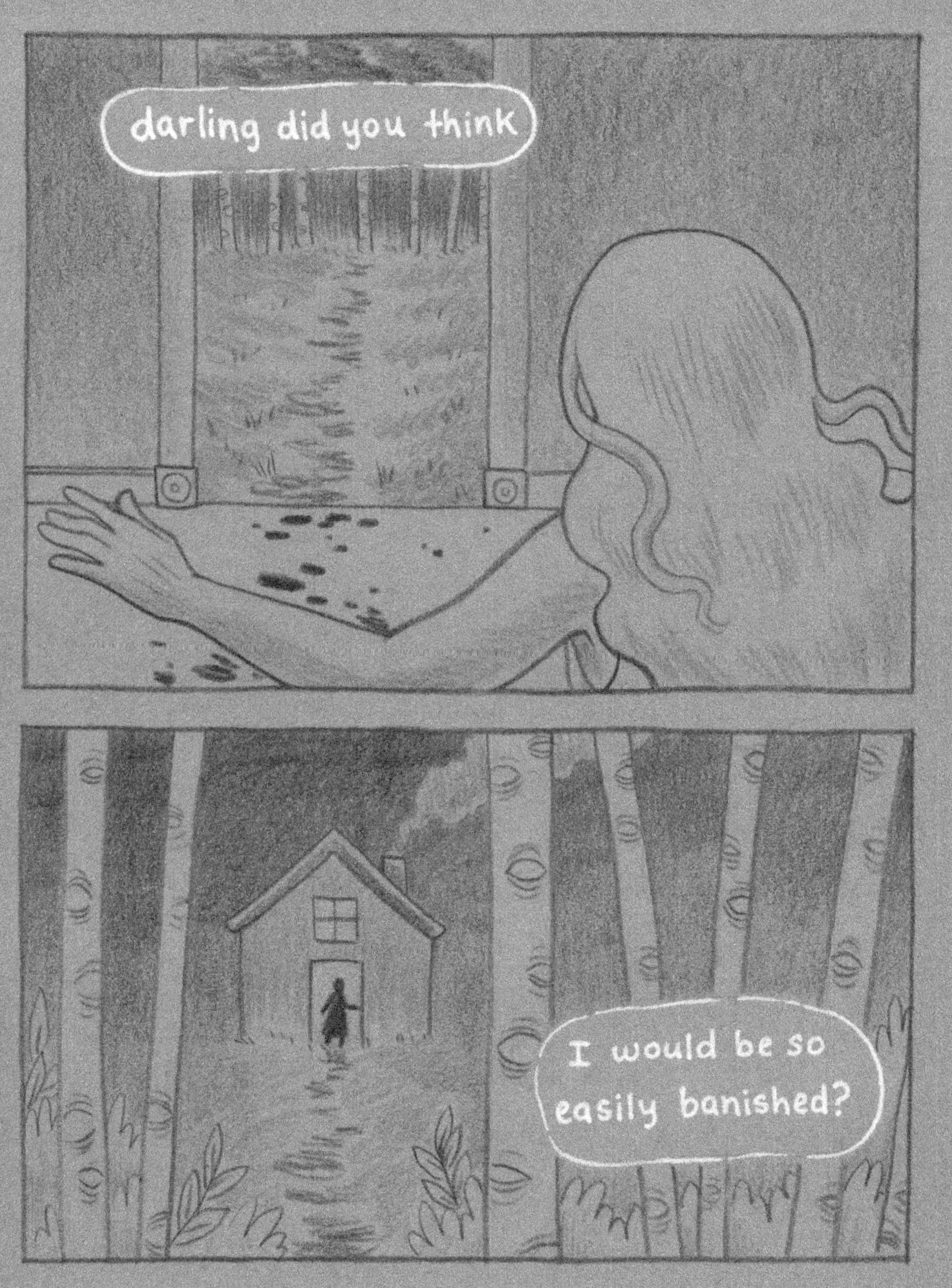
darling did you think
I would be so easily banished?

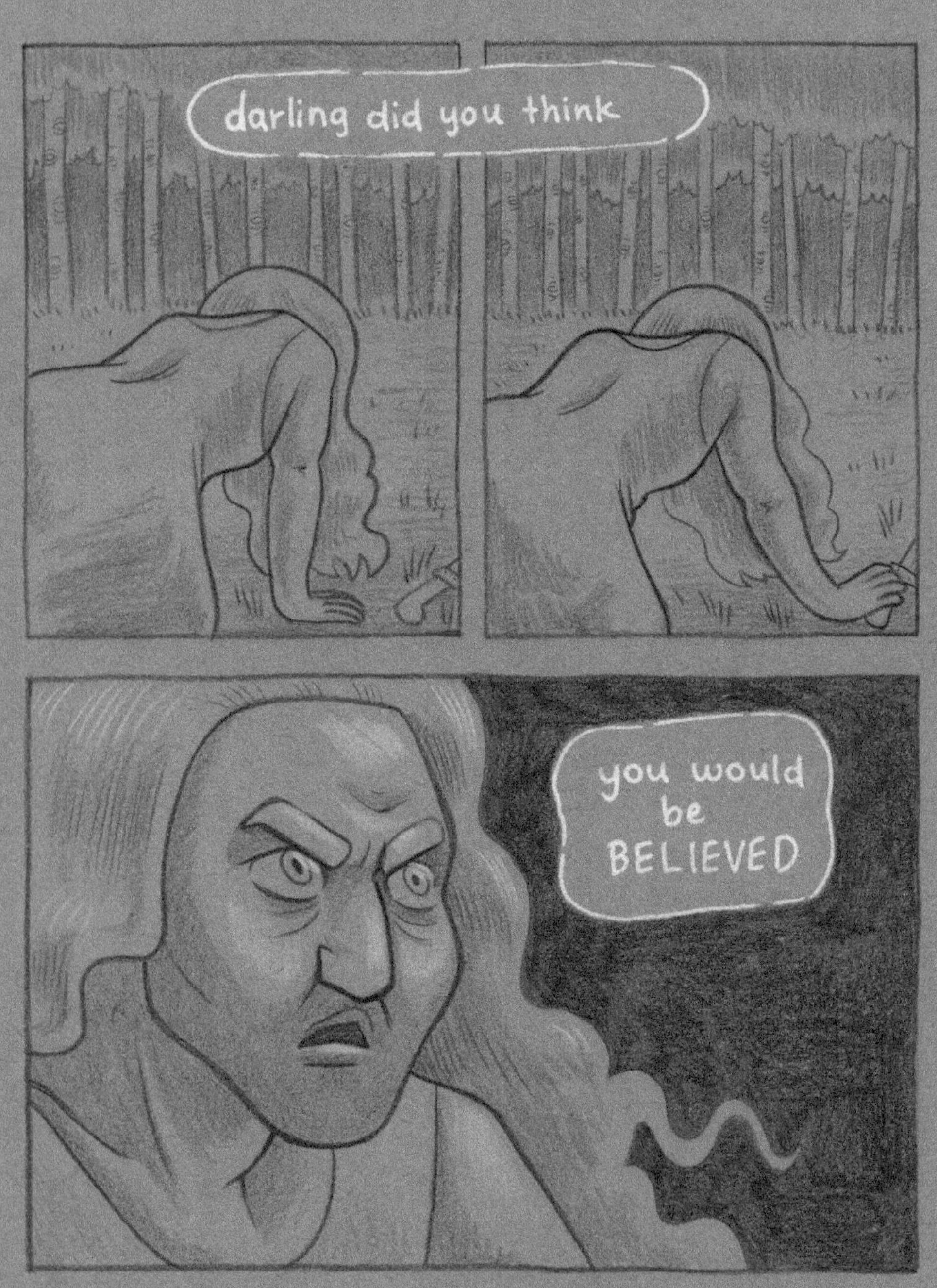
darling did you think
you would be BELIEVED

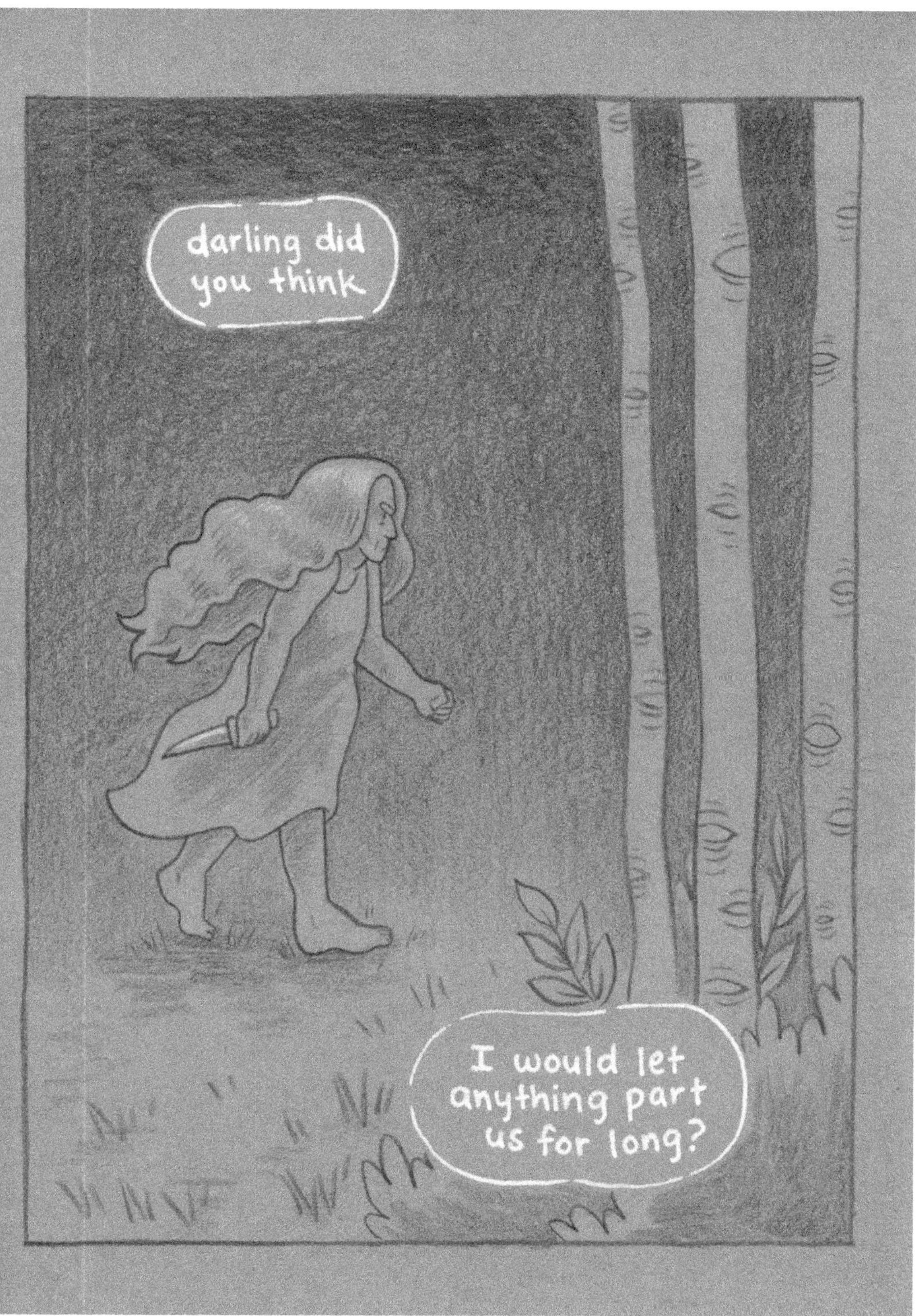
darling did you think
I would let anything part us for long?

The Ballet Master

Jennifer Habel

if you are lucky you still feel
him inside you are attuned
to what you know he wanted
dancers are like nuns they say
and in a way we were
the instruments of his creative powers
believe as we did and you are not
yourself any longer
where do you go from him
there was no comprehending
what he felt or thought he could
mold from you anything
he wanted *I know where you were*
I know what you ate I know
where you slept he was our conscience
the most exciting relationship
was with him his hands
on our necks our legs our backs what
would he do next
everyone was watching
dancers are like wine sweet
before they ripen
then vinegar he said old dancers
they should just go away
and die we didn't have to speak
he saw what was inside us
it might be enough to live
a whole life on if you are lucky
you still feel him inside you my place is
with ghosts he said I'm not old
I've just lived a long time

Weyland-Yutabi Has Its Hands Over My Mouth

Jodi Hooper

is a monster
a monster
if it makes you
money?

if it goes
to college and swims
or plays basketball?

is it a monster
if you're married
progeny bursting
tearing you
all blood?

is it not born
as we are screaming
wet
smooth carapace
not yet formed—

is it not soft
then?
can you make
a monster

on purpose?
hold it
in your arms
and sing
lullabies
of conquest

of acid blood ringing
screams
from supple
throats?

if you whisper
weapons
into hands
do you hear
claws on metal
thick drool tightening
a noose?

can you feel breath
hot on your neck
its teeth in your womb?

does a monster shift
in the light
flickering a boy

in uniform
barbed-tailed too many
mouths
and back
again?

do exoskeleton
and suit
merge make
a judge's robes?

is a monster
a monster
if you love it
after
everything?

is a monster

a monster

if you let it be?

How I Confronted the Truth About My Fraternity's Racist History

Mike Ingram

In March of 2019, a photo surfaced of three Ole Miss fraternity brothers posing with guns beside a bullet-riddled memorial to Emmett Till, the Black teenager whose grisly 1955 murder was a flashpoint for the Civil Rights Movement. My stomach turned when I saw the picture, but I wasn't surprised. Twenty-odd years ago, I was in the same fraternity.

Kappa Alpha Order was founded in Lexington, Virginia, just after the Civil War. Its early members declared themselves "Southern in our loves" and "Aryan by blood." In 1923, the fraternity officially adopted Robert E. Lee as its "spiritual founder." Until recently, many chapters held Old South celebrations that included marches through campus in Confederate uniforms and "plantation-style balls" to which guests came dressed in antebellum attire, the men sporting Rhett Butler-style cravats and the women in frilly dresses with hoop skirts.

The chapter I joined at James Madison University never celebrated Old South, and I never saw any Confederate flags. Most of my fraternity brothers were from the D.C. suburbs or points farther north. But we had the requisite oil painting of Lee in our house, and I couldn't pretend to be wholly ignorant of KA's national reputation. In Charleston, South Carolina, where I spent much of my childhood, I knew a few adults who still talked fondly of their time in "the Order," and I grew up with a few guys who went on to pledge KA at Clemson and Wofford and Wake Forest. They owned brightly-colored pants and perfectly-weathered boat shoes. They had names like Trey and Tripp, and Tradd.

Over winter break of my freshman year, I ran into one of those guys at a party, and he seemed surprised to learn we'd joined the same fraternity. "No offense," he said, "but you don't really strike me as the type."

I wasn't. At least not at Clemson, or Ole Miss, or UVA. I doubt those chapters would've had me, even if I'd wanted to join. The chapter at JMU was a small upstart, and while we weren't exactly *Revenge of the Nerds*, we weren't the Omegas from *Animal House*, either. Though I wonder: Was that part of the appeal? Like sneaking into the country club through a back entrance, disguised as the help. In Charleston, I played tennis with some of those T-named boys and went to church with others, but I was never truly a part of their world. After tennis practice, they went off to cotillion and I went home to watch *Gilligan's Island* reruns. After eighth grade, their parents sent them to private schools downtown. Their families were from Charleston, whereas mine only lived there. I remember going to a classmate's house in sixth grade for a group project and his mother asking where I was from. I told her the name of our subdivision, and she laughed. "No, dear, your family," she said. "Where are they from?"

I hated all that snobby posturing. But I also spent enough time on the peripheries of old-money Charleston society to be fascinated by it. Not that pledging

KA would make me a member of the South's landed gentry, but at least they'd have to let me into their parties.

I graduated high school in 1994. That year, the Ocala Star-Banner ran a story about the University of Florida's KA chapter, including an interview with one of its African-American members. Asked what motivated him to join a fraternity with roots in the Confederacy, he said, "If you hang around here, they are always talking about Lee. What he stood for is what we stand for. You conduct yourself as a gentleman at all times. That's colorblind."

If you'd asked me about the Lee portrait in our fraternity house back in my college days, I would've said the same thing. Maybe I would've pointed to our chapter's Black members. Maybe I would have told you my favorite story about Lee, passed down from one of the older guys, about the time he took communion with a Black man, in Richmond, after the war. In the version I heard, the young man came bounding down the aisle of St. Paul's and then knelt at the altar, to the befuddlement of the congregation—many of whom, like Lee, were descended from Virginia's landed gentry. The Episcopalian priest froze, unsure of what to do. But then Lee came walking down the aisle, head bowed. He knelt beside the young man and nodded to the priest, who continued with the service.

That was the version of Lee I liked. Stoic. Kind. Always carrying himself with quiet dignity. That version reminded me of my father, who was also a career military officer with a humble bearing. Of course, my dad never led an armed insurrection against the United States in defense of slavery. But my pledge manual assured me that Lee was a reluctant Civil War general, that he had no love for the institution of slavery but was "compelled by his great sense of duty" to follow his home state out of the Union. After the war, "Lee held no bitterness, nor did he indulge in self-pity." Instead, he accepted the presidency of Washington College (now Washington and Lee), where his life intersected with the lives of KA's founders. To them, Lee "personified the heroic knights of the past, representing their noblest ideals and traditions of chivalrous behavior." My pledge manual's chapter on Lee's life, in fact, is titled "The Last Gentle Knight."

I realize how ridiculous all that sounds. But at 18, it dovetailed rather neatly with the story I'd learned as a kid in Charleston, where you could still find plenty of people who used the phrase *War of Northern Aggression* without apparent irony. On school field trips to plantations, we learned the differences between "good" slave masters and "bad" ones (curiously, the masters of the plantations we were touring always fell into the "good" category). My eighth-grade South Carolina History textbook took pains to de-emphasize slavery as the chief cause of the war, instead leaning into a Lost Cause narrative of states' rights and unchecked federal power.

It's not fair to portray myself as some gullible idiot; I was a smart kid with access to a university library. With a little digging, I could have discovered that even that communion story was probably bullshit. The original version appeared in the *Richmond Times-Dispatch* in 1905, some 40 years after it supposedly happened, and was later reprinted in a magazine called *Confederate Veteran*. In that version, the story is given a different meaning. The young Black man enters the church to "offend and humiliate" its white congregation by flaunting his new freedom. But Lee refuses to take the bait. Instead, he ignores the man completely, which allows the service to continue "as if the negro had not been present."

Several years ago, I was talking to my then-girlfriend about my fraternity days. By then, I'd developed a set of stock answers to the inevitable questions. Yes, the Lee thing was problematic, but no one in our chapter took it seriously, and anyway, it wasn't really about the Civil War or even the South. "It was about being gentlemen," I said. "You know, chivalry and all that."

The look she gave me: I can still see it. Maybe I should mention that she was working on a Ph.D. in history; she's now a professor. "You realize those things are all connected," she said. "The whole cult of Lee, and chivalry and knighthood, and the Civil War as this noble lost cause?"

I don't remember what I said then. I probably hemmed and hawed for a while or tried to change the subject with a dumb joke. Eventually, I must have admitted she was right because of course, she was. But college had been a long time ago. I was only a kid. Who could possibly care anymore?

Then Charlottesville happened.

On the morning of August 12, 2017, I opened Twitter and saw images of white men brandishing tiki torches. My first thought was that they looked like frat boys. My second thought was that UVA's actual frat boys would be pissed when they discovered Home Depot was out of tiki torches. How were they supposed to light their backyard parties?

Then I read more, and it stopped being funny.

The Unite the Right rally brought together a rogues' gallery of white supremacist groups, each with their own fringe beliefs and hate-filled causes. They'd chosen Charlottesville because of the city's decision, a few months earlier, to take down a statue of Robert E. Lee. As I watched footage of the rally, I wondered if any representatives of KA's national office had made the 45-minute drive from Lexington. I wondered if any current or former members of my fraternity's many Virginia chapters, including my own, were there to throw their support behind Lee's legacy. I wondered if they would insist, the way I used to, that it had nothing to do with race.

An early draft of this essay began with the line, "I was once a member of a white supremacist organization." It struck me as too hyperbolic, too clickbaity, but is it untrue?

For nearly its entire history, KA has done its part to fight against racial justice in America. Samuel Zenas Ammen, the fraternity's "practical founder," who wrote the secret ritual and codified KA's creeds and beliefs, openly praised the Klan, writing in 1922 that both organizations—founded in the same year—were "reactions against the same evils." The fraternity's elaborate Old South celebrations didn't flourish until the 1950s, when college campuses across the South were facing pressure to integrate. When the University of Georgia finally admitted its first Black student in 1964, the KA house flew its Confederate flag at half-mast. In 2010, at the University of Alabama, a parade of KAs in Confederate uniforms paused their march in front of the Alpha Kappa Alpha house, where members of the historically Black sorority and their families were celebrating the chapter's 35th anniversary.

KA's national office would probably point out that they've since banned

Confederate uniforms. That they've discouraged chapters from holding Old South. That the chapter at Ole Miss expelled those four members caught in the photo. Though as recently as 2016, based on publicly available Facebook posts, the Ole Miss chapter was still playing antebellum dress-up at its annual formal, which they renamed the Rose Ball. That year, it was held at a plantation in Louisiana, one that just happened to be a principal filming location for *Twelve Years a Slave*.

I have no interest in defending my former fraternity. I'm not interested in defending my decision to join, either. But I am interested in understanding that decision. At 18, I considered myself politically progressive and actively anti-racist. I was one of those college students who made their parents listen to dinner-table lectures on social justice. So how did I maintain such a blind spot in this one area of my life? How did I walk into a frat house, see a painting of Lee on the wall, and not immediately walk back out?

Two years before Charlottesville, a white supremacist named Dylann Roof marched into the Emanuel African Methodist Episcopal Church in Charleston and opened fire, killing nine people. That church is four miles from the Lutheran church I grew up attending, the congregation of which was nearly all-white. Martin Luther King, Jr.'s observation that Sunday worship is the most segregated hour in American life still holds true in many places. Across the street from my old church, perched atop a 115-foot pedestal, sits a likeness of John C. Calhoun, one of the South's most virulent defenders of slavery. I'm sure we learned about Calhoun in school, but to me, he was only a name, one more vaguely important historical figure.

Other Charlestonians had a harder time ignoring the monument. In her 1983 memoir, Mamie Garvin-Fields, an African-American educator and activist born in Charleston in 1888, says she couldn't help but take the statue personally. "Our white city fathers wanted to keep what Calhoun stood for alive," she writes. She describes the experience of passing by and feeling Calhoun looking her in the face and telling her to stay in her place. She goes on to say that whenever she and her friends passed through the park, they'd carry a few stones in their pockets to chuck at the monument: "Whites had to come and put him way up high, so we couldn't get to him."

After the Emanuel AME murders, someone spray-painted "racist" on the base of the statue, which became one more touchpoint in the ongoing debate about the future of Confederate monuments and memorials across the South. Though we should remember it's not a new debate, even if some of us—myself included—only woke up to it in recent years. In 1971, Gloria Steinem spoke at the University of Missouri, and she pointed to two symbols that she said represented the exclusion Black students felt on campus: the Confederate Rock, a Civil War memorial dedicated in the '30s, and the Confederate flag that was flying, even as she spoke, outside the KA house.

I'm still friends with a number of my former fraternity brothers, and I don't regret spending my college years hanging out with them. I just wish we'd done so under the auspices of another organization, or no organization at all. Why not rent a house, throw parties, take camping trips, without 130 years of white supremacist baggage following us around?

I don't mean to be flip. Researching and writing this essay has made me think seriously about my relationship to white supremacy, a term that in 1994 I would have associated with only the most virulent skinheads and neo-Nazis. But white supremacy was embedded in the lessons I learned in school, and in the aristocratic power structures of old-money Charleston, and in the willful ignorance I practiced every time I tried to shrug away my fraternity's ugly history. For white supremacy to exist, it needs generals and foot soldiers, but it also needs people who are willing to look the other way. It needs people who would rather not talk about it, who would rather not investigate their own culpability and associations and blind spots. For too long, I was one of those people. But I'm trying—earnestly, if belatedly—to not be one anymore.

Piranha Plop

Vanessa Couto Johnson

A piranha sits

on top of my kitchen cabinet like the Cheshire Cat,
open-mouthed grin as I cook.

He came from my ancestors' waters

into my mother's suitcase, into gift
for her mother-in-law, into gift from

my grandmother back to me.

In college, I showed my teeth
in imitation of his, both our faces to a camera.

I'm not sure where my keychain-size piranha

is now—body crisp and delicate; I may
have chipped off bits of fin when handling.

On a hunch, I open the wooden box with my name

and there it is: as red-bellied as ever, small
mouth open mid-chat. What a language

it would have learned if not dead as a babe.

I cannot hear the riddles of the kitchen piranha
or its recipe suggestions, while I'm sure

my rare steaks would be enjoyed. A movie,

though named *Piranha* (1978), has a plural
amount of rubber puppet fish

and was filmed up the road, a body

of water where I've shone flashlights on gar.
The film has a red herring of Claymation

fish walking on fin feet at the military facility. Sure,

why not: let genetic engineering benefit culinary entertainment,
Chef Pygocentrus Nattereri chuckling as contestants

compete on the new cooking show, *My Meal or I, Meal.*

The piranha judge chomping a loser's dish, then the loser.

My Collection of Monsters

Genevieve Mills

GIANT

The subway car was full of warm bodies pressing together. A tall man's heavy backpack pushed me on one side while a bulging briefcase pushed from the other. When the doors opened, and everyone elbowed out, I managed to snag a seat before the car refilled. The legs of the man next to me were spread wide and crossing the invisible border that marked my side of the seat. I uncrossed my ankles and let my legs fall apart, lined them up with my shoulders. The man didn't seem to notice our thighs pressing together. I wished to be taller, to have longer legs, to take up more space without worrying about inconveniencing anyone. There was a sharp pain in my right leg and then in my left, and the man gave me an irritated look as he put his knees together. My legs grew too large for him to ignore. I smiled. My head bumped against the top of the subway car. It smelled weird and probably hadn't been cleaned in years, I thought, as I had to tilt my head because I was still growing, and my face was pressing against the ceiling. People started to look up from their phones and pull out earbuds. "Sorry," I said, but didn't mean it. A screw burst out of the ceiling and hit the floor. The car seemed to be rocking more than usual. Metal screeched. Wind rushed through my hair as I broke through the top of the car. Luckily the train made another stop before I hit the top of the tunnel. Everyone ran out of the car I stood in, wobbling slightly as I tried to get used to my new center of gravity, and stared up at me from the platform. Someone called the cops. I kept growing, concrete crumbs hitting my chest. Some fell down my shirt, and I thought of how they would be annoying to fish out of my bra later. New York dirt didn't taste good, so I kept my lips pressed together, and my eyes shut as I shot through the earth. Before I reached the sidewalk, I heard screaming and cars honking. More concrete dust, coating my hair and skin light gray. I blinked in the sunlight. I kept growing. "Sorry," I said, again, and again. I didn't mean it.

ZOMBIE

I'm hungry for a new brain. This one is old, and when I lie in bed, I can feel the decay, smell the mildew growing along the edges of the wet matter. My dad can't donate blood because he was in Europe while Mad Cow disease was rampant. They don't have a blood test for it yet, they told him, so they don't know if he has it and he can't donate. "Thanks anyway, take a juice box." The internet says Mad Cow leads to spongelike holes in the brain, so I thought he'd know by now if he had it. But maybe you can't tell if there are holes in your brain. Maybe I inherited my father's potential disease, maybe my brain is slowly dissolving. A wet sponge full of holes resting in my skull, leaking gray dishwater. Maybe this hunger in my gut is a symptom. A new brain would solve everything.

WEREWOLF
I think I'd be much more productive if I were a monster for only one night a month.

VAMPIRE
As a child, I had chronic nosebleeds. I would wake up to the smell, then taste, of blood, the warmth already running down my chin. I would run to the bathroom with my hands cupped under my dripping face, then lean over the sink and watch the blood splash against the porcelain until the drops slowed. I didn't want to wake anybody up or let the blood stain anything. Then I'd take a box of tissues, lean back, and pinch my nose. Blood would clog my throat, and I'd cough over the sink. Eventually, I'd go back to sleep. I read in a novel that blood tasted like pennies, and I wasn't sure about that simile, so I picked the shiniest penny out of my mom's coin jar and stuck it in my mouth. It didn't taste like blood, I decided. Blood was earthier and more anxious.

GHOST
I would like all my exes to pine after me until the day they die. Even the men I just shared a kiss with in a crowded club. Even the woman I dated for two weeks and ghosted. Even the relationships that ended mutually. Even the ones who dumped me. Especially the ones who dumped me. I hope I haunt them. May they see my smile on other women's faces, my eyes when they close theirs at night. May they think of me when they watch the movies I liked, when they hear the songs, I danced to. May they always wonder what could have been. I want them to long for my touch. Let my name be their last words.

SIREN
On the last day of the cruise, the ocean was so calm it didn't look real. Like it was plastic or a dream, or it was the sky, and I was in an airplane looking out the window at dimpled clouds, not on the deck of a ship holding a plastic cup full of vodka and pineapple juice. "I just want to touch it. Maybe throw something, to make a splash," I said, and my friend, leaning against the railing next to me, nodded. I heard singing. The ocean pulsed. The singing was coming from somewhere far away. I pushed my stomach against the railing and imagined dropping my cup into the ocean and watching the ripples, but I felt too bad for all the dying animals below me to let go. I couldn't recognize the song. It was hot, and my skin was sticky with sweat. I wanted to know what the song was and who was singing. The ocean was fake. If I fell, I wouldn't sink, I would bounce. There was nothing around me, but the fake ocean and the singing, and I had to get closer to both. I ground my teeth together, flexed my feet. Then my friend touched my arm and said, "Let's go sit in the shade." As we walked away from the railing to lie down on some plastic lawn chairs, I realized the singing was coming from the drunk people by the pool.

SELKIE
When I left home behind and moved in with the man, I peeled off my skin and hid it. "You have to be someone else now," my mother told me. "Don't let him find your

old skin." So I hid my old skin in a safe deposit box at the bank and put the key next to my new apartment key on a metal loop. No one had to know I used to be a messy, mean person with ugly scarred skin. It was hidden away, and I resolved not to miss my home, which may have been more comfortable than the man's apartment, and warmer, but that home was behind me now. The man and I lived happily together. I learned how to cook and how to love. Sometimes in the shower, I ran my fingers along my skin, looking for scars that didn't exist, but overall, I was happy. Then the man didn't seem to be happy anymore. He was always restless and paced the apartment after he came home from work. Next to me in bed, he touched my face and asked if this was my real skin or if my old skin was more real. I pretended to fall asleep because I didn't know the answer. I became restless too. I went to the bank and opened my safe deposit box so I could check on my old skin. I found it then I remembered. When I got home that night, the man wasn't there, but I cooked dinner anyway and left a plate in the microwave for him. He came home late, smelling of lighter fluid, and kissed me hard against the kitchen counter. "What have you done?" I asked him. "I followed you to the bank," he said, and I felt sick. "We don't have to worry about your old skin anymore," he said. He kissed me again, and I kissed him back, tasting bile. "You're someone else now," he told me.

BANSHEE

I used to have night terrors where I was so scared, I couldn't scream. I wouldn't remember what the dreams were about. I would suddenly be awake and terrified, gasping for air and for a scream that wouldn't come. I would stare at my bedroom ceiling until my pulse slowed, and I could swallow the scream caught in my throat. I don't get night terrors anymore, but I'm sure if I were ever in a situation of fight or flight, where my life depended on fighting back or running, I would freeze. Awake and terrified, unable to even scream.

DRAGON

I would love to stop breathing fire. I keep my mouth shut as often as possible because I don't know what will come out when I open it. I feel a tickle in the back of my throat, the smell of charcoal, heat in my gut, and then there's a flame, blistering my lips. Sometimes people get out of the way in time, sometimes not. It would be much safer for everyone if I would just stop breathing fire, but I don't know how to stop. I have nightmares of one day emitting a flame so large it burns down everything I know, and I'm left alone in the ashes.

Contributors' Notes

EISUKE AIKAWA is a fiction writer based in Fukuoka, Japan. He has published two collections of short stories, *Haikingu* (2017) and *Kumo wo hanareta tsuki* (2018). His short fiction has appeared in venues such as *Bungakukai*, *Hidden Authors*, and *Taberu no ga osoi*. His first novel is *Hannah no inai jugatsuwa* (2020). TOSHIYA KAMEI holds an MFA in Literary Translation from the University of Arkansas. His recent translations have appeared in venues such as *Clarkesworld*, *Cosmic Roots & Eldritch Shores*, and *The Magazine of Fantasy & Science Fiction*.

ZACK BEAN is the author of the story collection *Man on Fire* (ELJ, 2016). His stories and essays have appeared in *Fiction*, *Pank*, *Miracle Monocle*, and elsewhere. He teaches creative writing at Montana State University in Bozeman, Montana, where he lives with his family and their pets.

JEN FAWKES is the author of *Mannequin and Wife* (LSU Press), named one of Largehearted Boy's Favorite Short Story Collections of 2020. Her second book, *Tales the Devil Told Me*, won the 2020 Press 53 Award for Short Fiction and is forthcoming in October 2021. Her fiction has won numerous prizes, from *The Pinch, Salamander, Washington Square Review*, and others, and has appeared in *One Story, Lit Hub, Crazyhorse, The Iowa Review, The Rumpus, Best Small Fictions* 2020, and many other venues. She lives in Little Rock, Arkansas, with her husband and several imaginary friends. "Hobbled" has previously appeared in *The Southeast Review* and *Mannequin and Wife*.

MELANIE GILLMAN is a cartoonist who specializes in LGBTQ books for kids and teens. They are the creator of the webcomic and graphic novel *As the Crow Flies*, published in 2017 by Iron Circus Comics, and winner of the 2018 Stonewall Honor Award. Their newest book, *Stage Dreams*, was published by Lerner/Graphic Universe in 2019. They are also a senior lecturer in the Comics MFA Program at the California College of the Arts.

JENNIFER HABEL is the author of *The Book of Jane*, winner of the Iowa Poetry Prize, and *Good Reason*, winner of the Stevens Poetry Manuscript Competition. Her poems have appeared in *The Sewanee Review*, *The Believer*, *Gettysburg Review*, *Gulf Coast*, and elsewhere. She lives in Cincinnati. "The Ballet Master" has previously appeared in *Barrow Street* and *The Book of Jane*.

JODI HOOPER is a poet, fiction writer, and 2020 graduate of the University of Louisville. Her work explores themes of the body and the fraught experience of human connection by way of 80's sci-fi movies, carnivorous plants, vampirism, and the ever-closing gap between monster and man. Jodi's poetry has most recently appeared in Folx Gallery's *Absolute Pleasure* exhibition and *Raptor Lit* magazine.

MIKE INGRAM is a writer, editor, podcaster, and English professor. His first book, *Notes from the Road*, is forthcoming from Awst Press in 2021. His stories and essays have appeared in a number of journals and magazines, including *Phoebe*, *North American Review*, *December*, *EPOCH*, *Southeast Review*, and *The Smart Set*. He's one of the founding editors of *Barrelhouse Magazine* and a co-host of the Book Fight podcast. "How I Confronted the Truth About My Fraternity's Racist History" has previously appeared in *Human Parts.*

VANESSA COUTO JOHNSON is the author of *Pungent dins concentric*, her first full-length book (Tolsun Books, 2018), and three chapbooks, most recently *speech rinse* (Slope Editions' 2016 Chapbook Contest winner). *Dialogist*, *Foundry*, *Softblow*, *Thrush*, and other journals and anthologies have published her poetry. A Brazilian born in Texas (a dual citizen), she has been a Lecturer at Texas State University since 2014.

GENEVIEVE MILLS lives in New York and is pursuing an MFA at Sarah Lawrence College. Her work has appeared in *Matchbook*, *Storm Cellar Quarterly*, *Jellyfish Review*, *Psychopomp Magazine*, *Crab Fat Magazine*, and *Drunk Monkeys*, among others.

Miracle Monocle thanks you for the purchase of this book. We hope that you enjoyed it and will support future titles released in conjunction our new publishing initiative: *The* Miracle Monocle *Micro-Anthology Series.* All proceeds from the sale of this book will go toward the realization of future titles in this series. Founded in 2009 as an annual digital literary journal, *Miracle Monocle* is now an AWP-award-winning biannual journal, as well as a training program for students with ambitions in the field of publishing, and a nexus of literary programming in Louisville, Kentucky. We pride ourselves on serving as a home for innovative literary art that might otherwise go unnoticed in a crowded media landscape; we are also committed to showcasing writers who might regularly escape the attention of traditional or commercial publishers. We take pleasure in juxtaposing emerging talent with established voices. For readers interested in learning more about *Miracle Monocle*, or writers who might be interested in joining the ranks of our contributors, we invite you to visit us online: louisville.edu/miraclemonocle

www.ingramcontent.com/pod-product-compliance
Lightning Source LLC
LaVergne TN
LVHW010546100826
845148LV00013B/2631

* 9 7 8 1 7 3 4 1 2 3 3 1 9 *